STUDIES IN ENGLISH LITERATURE
Volume LXXI

D0843973

CHRISTIAN THEOLOGY
AND
OLD ENGLISH POETRY

by

JAMES H. WILSON

1974
MOUTON
THE HAGUE · PARIS

PR
203
.W5

LIBRARY OF CONGRESS CATALOG CARD NUMER: 74-78921

Printed in The Netherlands by Mouton & Co., The Hague

For R. M. Lumiansky

TABLE OF CONTENTS

I

THE BACKGROUND

The Old English poetic tradition begins with the poem *Widsith* (c. 650) and extends through the battle poem *Maldon*, which is dated 991 because of the fact that mention of the battle appears in the *Anglo-Saxon Chronicle* under the entry for that year. It is impossible to say how much poetry was written during this period, but some 30,000 lines of epic, elegy, and lyric, as well as epic treatment of saints' lives have survived. We are sure that most of the extant poetry was written between 650 and 900, and that little of it is of later composition than the third quarter of the ninth century. The difficulty, not to say impossibility, of exact dating makes any such statement somewhat speculative, but, generally speaking, this 250-year period is that of the most intense poetic creation. Of the many scholarly problems which have arisen concerning this body of work, the most persistent to date has been the question of the nature and extent of the influence of Christian theology upon it. Although such scholars as Klaeber, Ehrismann, and O. S. Anderson earlier in this century suggested Christian and allegorical interpretations of the poetry, it was not until about 1950 that such suggestions gained any wide acceptance. Since 1950 the idea that Old English poetry is a part of the medieval allegorical tradition has rapidly come to the fore. It is this idea which I shall investigate. Such a study will necessitate looking carefully at the several genres in which medieval poetry appears and the treatment of individual poems within these genres; however, before such a treatment can be undertaken, it will be necessary to say some things generally about the body of work and its background.

Old English poetry is a part of the literary heritage of the North and West Germanic peoples, those peoples living in northern Europe along the Baltic Sea, in Scandinavia, including Iceland, and in England. It is generally recognized as the most important body of work produced by these peoples, challenged only by the work in Old Norse. The raw material of Old English poetry is, in large part, made up of the history and legends of these Germanic peoples as such materials were handed down by the singer, whose job it was to learn and pass on knowledge of great men and events. Many of the events about which Old English poems center took place on the continent long before the migration of the tribes to their island home in England. The epic *Beowulf* is, of course, the prime example of this use of continental history and legend: the main character is not English, nor do any of the events in the poem take place in England. This use of Continental rather than native English material in the poetry has provided much of the ground from which scholars have argued for the essential heathen nature of the work.

We do not know a great deal about the Germanic peoples of northern Europe in the centuries immediately preceding their migration to England. Tacitus provides us with the most direct contact we have with them, but it must be kept in mind that Tacitus may not have been writing from first hand observation and that he wrote toward the end of the first century A.D., three-and-a-half centuries before the invasions of England began. Changes are likely to take place, even in a conservative culture, during such a length of time. Tacitus tells us that the Germanic peoples were semi-nomadic, agricultural, and warlike. He tells us that they had a high conception of personal honor and allegiance to an accepted leader (the *comitatus* system), and that they had as early as the first century developed the system of *wergild* as a means of avoiding feuds which could dangerously disrupt their whole social structure, a structure built around the family unit. They celebrated, he tells us, an earth-born god, Tuisco, claimed that Hercules had once visited them, and that they sang of Hercules as first among their heroes as they went into battle. Of particular interest is

Tacitus' remark that the celebration of their god is "in their ancient songs, their only way of remembering or recording the past".

By means of such oral transmission much of the early Germanic culture was passed along into Old English poetry: from *Widsith* we hear of Eormanric, Attila, Alboin; from *Beowulf*, of Hygelac, Hrothgar, Finn, Ingeld; and we have also the fragments concerning Walthar of Aquitaine and Finnesburg. All of these men and places figure in the continental history of the peoples whose descendants settled England in the fifth and sixth centuries, and they became the raw material upon which much of the poetry of the Old English written tradition is necessarily based.

It is impossible to say just what influence their contact with Roman culture had on the Germanic peoples during the centuries prior to their migration to England. Tacitus' statement that they are a people "aboriginal, and not mixed at all with other races through immigration or intercourse" suggests a solitary and conservative character which, taken together with their warlike nature, would have resisted encroachment from outside of any peoples or ideas. The possibility of Christian influence in the northern areas has been suggested, although it is fairly certain that the Franks and the Saxons in the far North remained relatively untouched.[1] The reaction of the eighth-century descendants of these northern Germanic peoples against Boniface, whom they slaughtered along with his entire company in 753, attests the fact that on the continent the old prejudices died hard. By this same date, on the other hand, the descendants of these peoples who had migrated to England had been Christians for more than 100 years.

Linguistic evidence shows that the Roman culture had not been entirely unfelt among the northern tribes. The Germanic settlers of England brought with them a stock of words pertaining to war, trade, or household items which they had borrowd from Latin on the continent. Baugh makes a conservative estimate of perhaps 50 conquest Latin words in Old English; Mary Serjeantson suggests a

[1] Representative statements may be compared in Edward Maslin Hulme, *The Middle Ages* (New York, 1929), pp. 166-169, and Williston Walker, *A History of the Christian Church* (New York, 1946), p. 130.

list of about 170.[2] Although the words borrowed during this period
show practically no direct association with religious concepts, the
very fact of the borrowing itself opens the possibility for speculation as to the influence of missionaries on the tribes, for it is not
to be doubted that missionaries accompanied merchants into newly
occupied Roman provinces, especially after 313 when Constantine's
edict of toleration made possible much greater missionary activity.
Missionary zeal had been one of the distinguishing characteristics
of the church, of course, even before the edict. We have the early
Christianization of England and Ireland as substantiation of this
fact. Of course, in the light of the reaction against Boniface, even
though the Franks and Saxons had had at least some exposure to
Roman Christian culture over a period of 200 years, we cannot
say with much authority that Christianity had made any lasting
impression upon these people, but the swiftness of the conversion
of these same people once they had settled in England raises the
question of possible prior conditioning.

On the other hand, we are certain that long before the Germanic
invasions of the island a church had existed in both England and
Ireland. Although it is difficult to deal with the Romano-British
and Irish churches separately, it is important that the Irish church
be dealt with first, since it represents a continuous influence in the
development of Anglo-Saxon culture. The earliest date at which
Christianity was present in Ireland is debatable, but it is fairly
certain that it was there as early as the fourth century, having come
from the Middle East by way of western Gaul and Britain. Such
early western movement of the church is well established by the
existence of a church at Lyons probably as early as the third quarter of the second century. Eusebius, in his *Ecclesiastical History*,
records martyrdoms at Lyons in the year 177. We also know that
there must have been a church established in Britain as early as the
late third century, for in 314 three British bishops attended the
Council or Arles. Tertullian and Origen imply that the church

---

[2]   Albert C. Baugh, *A History of the English Language*, 2nd ed. (New York,
1957), p. 91; Mary A. Serjeantson, *A History of Foreign Words in English*
(New York, 1962), pp. 271-288.

reached Britain as early as the beginning of the third century.[3] At any rate, it seems safe to assume that the missionary zeal of the early church carried it across Gaul to Britain and on to Ireland at an early date.

It is not so much the mere presence of the church in Ireland at an early date that is important to the development of the Old English poetic tradition; it is, rather, the fundamental character of the church that was established there. Originally, the Irish church, like the earliest church settlements of Gaul at Lerins and Tours, had an organization similar to the eastern system of autonomous monasteries, a system which leaned away from the centralizing tendency of the Roman diocesan pattern. Monasticism in the pre-Benedictine church was essentially a carry-over of the ascetic reaction of third- and fourth-century churchmen against the secularizing influence of the more sophisticated urban centers of the faith, particularly that of Rome, an asceticism which still found expression in the seventh century in the withdrawal of St. Cuthbert to his hut on Farne Island. To be sure, the church since as early as the second century had begun to develop a system of dioceses, based on the Roman civil structure, with a bishop over each diocese, but monasticism is an entirely different development. The first monastics were the desert fathers who established autonomous settlements, each ruled by an abbot. Apparently any recognition of a central governing power over such settlements, wide-spread as they were, was of an exclusively spiritual, not to say mystic, nature and necessarily vague. Such settlements as Lerins and Tours, although St. Martin, like his predecessor Hilary of Poitiers, was consecrated a bishop, were essentially monastic and therefore carried with them much of the ascetic atmosphere of their eastern forerunners. It was this monasticism that made its way to Ireland through the semi-legendary Palladius and through St. Patrick, who studied at Lerins. It would seem reasonable to assume also that if the third- and fourth-century Roman church in England had any organization at all, it, as well as the Irish church, would have reflected the pre-Benedictine monastic ideal.

[3] John Lingard, *The History and Antiquities of the Anglo-Saxon Church*, 2nd ed., 2 vols. (London, 1858), I, 4 n.

When the Germanic invasions of the British Isles began, the Irish church was isolated from the continent while the church in England was being all but destroyed or pushed into Wales and Ireland. After the first success of the invasions, the Romano-British church might be said to have co-existed with the Irish church in Wales and Ireland, where the two grew even closer to sameness. Archeological findings indicate that the Romano-British church survived even in England as late as the end of the fifth century. The point important to the study of the Old English poetry is that the Christianity, which returned to England in the sixth century after the Germanic occupation was complete, came from Ireland and Wales. Benedictine influence did not appear in England until 597 and had no real influence until the second quarter of the seventh century when Paulinus succeeded in the conversion of Edwin of Northumbria.

It is certain that Christianity was in Ireland before the ministry of St. Patrick, which began about 431. Keating in his *General History of Ireland* records King Cormac Macart's renunciation of druidism in 266 and refusal to be buried with his idolatrous kinsmen. Palladius, also, is said to have preceded Patrick. Granting the possibility that the story of King Cormac Macart is apocryphal, the safest assumption seems to be that the religion arrived in the island in the fourth century from western Gaul and Britain. St. Patrick, born toward the end of the fourth century in Britain, was, according to his *Confession*, the son and the grandson of Christian churchmen. At 16 he was captured by marauding Scots and taken as a prisoner to Ireland. After escaping he made his way to Gaul, where he probably studied at Lerins and later, on a second trip, at Auxerre. Both places, being monastic settlements, were centers of eastern influence. It is possible that Auxerre was the school to which many Irish monks went for study and therefore heavily influenced the eastern form which the Irish church took under Patrick and later.

The eastern autonomous monastic structure found itself much at home among the Irish. From earliest times, the Irish system of government had been established on the basis of small autonomously ruled tribal units. Either a tribal chief and his followers would be converted and thus establish the tribal territorial limits as the authority of the church or monastic settlement, or a converted chief would make territorial grants to a churchman, similarly establishing the limits of his authority. Within such a politically unstable structure, a church built on the principle of a central authority such as that of the Roman church would have been unthinkable. Hence, the Irish church took on the structure of autonomous monasteries, a structure paralleling the governmental structure of the island. Of course, there were other deviations from Roman custom: the computation of the date of Easter which the Irish church had inherited through its roots in the eastern rite, and the wearing of the Druidic tonsure, but these deviations did not become important until the Irish and Roman churches came into direct conflict in England in the seventh century. Just how much of a monastic structure existed in Ireland before St. Patrick's arrival has been questioned. Two facts, however, argue heavily in favor of the existence of such a structure in the pre-Patrick church: the fact, discussed just above, that the governmental structure of the island would have made any but a monastic-type settlement all but impossible, and, second, the rapidity with which Patrick proceeded to establish monasteries throughout the island, all conforming to the eastern system.

The Irish church exhibited another important characteristic of the eastern settlements, one which was also seen in the first monastic establishments in Gaul, such as Lerins, and which was to play an important role in the development of one of the traditional themes of Old English poetry — the tradition of the *peregrinus*, the solitary monk who made his lonely way into the new and, in many instances, hostile lands in order to preach the new religion.[4] The church had made its way from the Near East across Europe along pathways beaten largely by the *peregrini*. These men usually separated themselves from a parent monastery in groups of 13, symbolizing Christ and His 12 disciples, and established themselves in

---

[4] For a discussion of the terms *peregrinus* or *peregrinatio*, see James F. Kenney, *The Sources for the Early History of Ireland*, 2 vols. (New York, 1929), I, 488-489.

or along the borders of heathen lands.[5] They would build their huts and then fan out individually into the new territory carrying the message of salvation. The story of St. Columba and his settlement on Iona is typical of this kind of operation. These men represented much of the great missionary strength of the new Church. Such men were, in all probability, the first to bring Christianity to Ireland from the settlement in Roman England. During the sixth, seventh, and eighth centuries, *peregrini* from Ireland and from the new Anglo-Saxon church, which itself was largely a result of the missionary work of Irish monks, returned to reconvert all central Europe when the church had fallen on lean days there. The great names in the reestablishment of the church in England after the Germanic invasions were those of Columba, Aidan, Eata, Colman, and Cuthbert; in the reconversion of central Europe we know of the work of such men as Willibrord, Boniface, Sturm, Leoba, Lebuin, and Willibald. The way of the *peregrinus* did not die out, in spite of the nominal defeat of the Irish church at Whitby in 664.

What the *peregrinus* tradition gave to Old English poetry can best be termed an attitude toward life. We can call this attitude a willing acceptance of hardship in exchange for the consoling hope of eternal reward, an attitude inherited in large part from early patristic writing. It is the attitude which becomes the theme of the great elegiac poems of Old English, *The Wanderer, The Seafarer, The Ruin,* and perhaps *Deor.*

The fact can be too easily overlooked that until the fifth century there was a close cultural parallel between Ireland and England. Prior to the Germanic invasions of England both countries had been inhabited by the same peoples, the Celts with their druidic religion. In fact, some scholars believe that the pre-Christian gods of both countries were the same in spite of their slightly different names, differences which may be accounted for by rules of linguistic development.[6] The arrival of the Romans in force in 43 A.D. set the stage for the influence of the Christian church in the islands. The church did not come with the first settlements, of

---

[5] Note here the medieval tendency to see all experience symbolically. This tendency will become important later in this chapter.
[6] Charles Squire, *Celtic Myth and Legend* (London, n.d.), p. 42. Also see John Rhys, *Studies in the Arthurian Legend* (Oxford, 1891), *passim.*

course, since it was still at that period confined to a small area of the Middle East where the apostles were just beginning to preach, but it is certain that it reached the island even before the edict of toleration in 313, since we have already mentioned the presence of the British bishops at Arles in 314. If the church was established in England by that early date, it is safe to assume that some missionary work must have been done in Ireland as early as the beginning of the fourth century and that a church began to take form there shortly thereafter. The important point is that a church did exist in both England and Ireland during the fourth and fifth centuries and that this fact argues also for the beginning growth in the islands of a Christian culture which had the better part of two centuries to develop before the Germanic invasions. Both these things taken together, the close cultural ties of the people and the length of time the church had had to develop, lead me to question the usual assumption, that the Christian priests made no attempt to carry on their work in the area of Germanic occupation.

This question, the continuity of the church in England during and after the invasions, poses what is felt to be the most difficult problem in any discussion of the influence of Christian theology on the development of Old English poetry. There can be no doubt that the continental invaders pushed a large part of the Romanized Celtic population out of the central section of the island, back into Cornwall, Wales, Scotland – even across the Irish Channel to Eire – and that they destroyed whatever of Roman architecture was used against them as military fortification, including the churches. The picture we are used to imagining, however, of the entire island's being put to the torch by bloodthirsty barbarians is rather far-fetched, particularly in view of the number of Roman remains which have apparently suffered more at the hands of time than of the Germans. Such descriptions of *eald enta geweorc* as we find in Old English poetry carry with them a sense of the magnificent that we associate not with the scorched and scattered rubble of battle but with the stubborn and gradual decay of great walls and gates and towers under the ravages of sleet and storm. Recent studies of the Germanic methods of occupation also make it clear that their advances were not always military, particularly after they had gained a firm foothold. In some instances tribes would simply move into new territory, clear land, and settle down to farm. In such instances they apparently lived in peace with neighboring Celts.[7] We have usually gone to Bede for accounts of the invasions and have pointed to his criticism in the *Ecclesiastical History*, I, xxii, of the Britons for their not having evangelized among the Germans, preferring apparently, to see them in hell. Another of Bede's statements in the same chapter, however, has been overlooked. He states specifically that Germanic tribesmen lived among the Celtic peoples and that Celtic priests maintained order among their people during the first generation after the invasions. It would appear from this statement that even though there may not have been active evangelizing among the invaders there was present a definite influence in the persons of the individual priests. It is certainly not beyond reason to suggest that, granted the missionary zeal of the early churchmen, these individual priests must have had some influence among the Germanic peoples who chose voluntarily to dwell in their midst. It is even slightly possible that the invaders might have heard in their new homes some of the same themes they and their ancestors had heard preached on the continent during the days of their first contact with Roman culture. The wide spread of Christianity among the Teutonic peoples is well documented. The Goths were Christianized by the fourth century and it has been said that their occupation of Rome in 410 was the real death blow to Roman paganism. It is an interesting coincidence that Quintus Aurelius Symmachus died in the same year.

To return to the question of England, most scholars until recently have proceeded on the assumption that Christianity was wiped out by the invaders, that the culture which developed in the island after the invasions was pagan and barbarous, and, more important, that it remained so for more than 300 years; at least, these inferences must be made if we accept the frequent scholarly insistence on the pagan nature of the poetry produced in England as late as A.D. 750 or later and the crudity of the religious verse written

---

[7] See R. H. Hodgkin, *A History of the Anglo-Saxons*, 2 vols., 3rd ed. (London, 1952), I, chap. 5, especially pp. 175ff. Although definite proof is impossible, there is evidence to support the conclusion that such coexistence and absorption did take place.

much later. As I have pointed out, there seems sufficient evidence for assuming that this case has been overstated, for in the light of the evidence concerning the nature of the invasions brought forth above, it seems to follow that the Germanic tribesmen were to some slight degree prepared for the coming of the Irish monks in the North during the latter half of the sixth century and for the advent of the Augustinian mission which touched upon the Isle of Thanet in 597. The possibility of this prior conditioning is strengthened by the swiftness with which these predominantly pagan peoples became converted to Christianity once they had become settled in the island. Christianity had been accepted by practically all of the invaders within 100 years of the completion of the occupation. Such rapid conversion would also seem to indicate a much stronger church organization at work in the island during the entire period of the invasions than we have hitherto been willing to admit, an organization which suffered bitterly at the hands of the invaders but was not destroyed. The proximity of the Welsh and Irish monasteries further substantiates the possibility. There is some question as to the continuity of the Welsh monasteries after the withdrawal of the Roman legions, but even if these centers were temporarily abandoned and a new church organization received via the sea lanes from western Gaul in the fifth century, as has been suggested, the organization flourished during the period of the invasions. Since no such question exists of a break in the continuity of the Irish church since the late fourth of early fifth century, it seems not unreasonable to suggest, in the face of all this evidence, the possibility of a continuous religious influence upon the continental invaders, an influence which would have been highly instrumental in their rapid conversion once their invasions were complete.

1. THE INFLUENCE OF SAINT AUGUSTINE OF HIPPO

In the preceding pages much has been said about the monastic structure of the early church, about its missionary zeal, and about the *peregrini*, who carried the church from the Middle East across

Europe and into the islands of England and Ireland. Now we turn to a discussion of certain aspects of its theological development which play a large part in the growth of western culture and in the context for Old English poetry.

Early in its life the Christian church was thrown seriously on the defensive, on the one hand by Roman accusations of atheism and anarchy and worse, and, on the other hand, by the rise of strong anti-Catholic sects such as the Manichaeans, Arians, and Pelagians. In such a position churchmen found it increasingly necessary to develop in some permanent form the theological stand of the church. This attempt began with the work of the apologists in the early second century and culminated in the great works of SS. Jerome and Augustine of Hippo in the late fourth and early fifth centuries. The work of St. Augustine is of special importance to the development of all early medieval literary theory and, therefore, is central to any discussion of the development of the poetic tradition in Old English. His works which bear directly upon the development of literary theory are the *De Magistro* and the *De Doctrina Christiana*. These works are important to the student of the Old English literary tradition because Pope Gregory the Great, being a devoted student of St. Augustine, imparted the Augustinian principles to Augustine of Canterbury, whom he sent to England in 597 to convert the Germanic tribesmen. Hence, there is a direct line from the work of St. Augustine to the poetry written in and around the monastic settlements in England beginning 50 or 60 years after the Roman mission reached the island.

Practically all of the writing from the middle of the second century to the time of St. Augustine (d. 430) was being done by Christian Latin writers and was didactic in nature. There was considerable study of the pagan classics along with the study of Holy Scripture but there was wide difference of opinion among churchmen as to the effect of the study of pagan writings on a devout Christian. St. Jerome's qualms of conscience over his love of Cicero are well-known; Pope Gregory the Great's letter to the bishop of Vienne lamenting his teaching of "ancient literature" is equally well-known, as well as Alcuin's chastizing of the monks of Lindisfarne. St. Augustine came to a different conclusion regarding the same problem, a conclusion which was to become generally accepted by the church:

> To study poets and philosophers with a view to making the wit more keen and better suited to penetrate the mystery of the Divine Word is to spoil the Egyptians of their treasure in order to build the tabernacle of God.[8]

Not only does this statement establish an attitude, it implies the method by which the attitude is to be supported – the allegorical method. The statement is an allegorical interpretation of the flight from Egypt, during which the Israelites took with them treasure in silver and gold but left behind the pagan idols. St. Augustine, in line with exegetical Christianizing of the Old Testament story, interpreted the silver and gold as the useful knowledge which could be gained from pagan writings, the idols as pagan superstition. The allegorical method had been in practice since the days of Philo, with whom it was apparently a means of reconciling Judaic with Hellenic teachings, but with the sanction given to it by St. Augustine it became the universal method of medieval biblical interpretation. All literature which was not literally in line with dogma came to be considered allegorical, or figurative, in order that through interpretation it could be brought into line with dogma, which policy contributed greatly to the essential didactic nature of all medieval writing in the Christian tradition. The allegorical interpretations of Virgil and Ovid which still found ready acceptance as late as the English Renaissance are prime examples of the moralizing tendency which the later Middle Ages inherited directly from the Christian apologists and other writers of the Christian Latin tradition of the first five centuries. Medieval etymologies and encyclopedic books show the same tendency when they assign allegorical significances to the various objects of nature. The medieval attitude which interpreted history as a series of events exemplifying the inevitable working out in human experience of the divine plan of God, and later fitted the genre of tragedy into the same mold, is in the line of descent from the allegorical-didactic tradition.

[8] Quoted in James Westfall Thompson and Edgar Nathaniel Johnson, *An Introduction to Medieval Europe* (New York, 1937), p. 221.

As a preface to any discussion of the writings of St. Augustine and his eventual effect on the Old English poetic tradition, it is necessary to make certain things clear. The first is that in the two treatises with which we shall deal, St. Augustine, in spite of his acceptance of the value of pagan writing, is primarily concerned with the literature of Holy Scripture and that when he deals with the pagan works he is doing so in order to establish contrasts between the pagan and the Christian writings. The second point is that to St. Augustine truth is the dogma of the church. There is never any doubt in his mind as to the essential nature of the truth which is to be discovered by a study of Scripture. He begins the *De Doctrina Christiana* with a significant statement bearing on this point:

1. There are two things necessary to the treatment of the Scriptures: a way of discovering those things which are to be understood, and a way of teaching what we have learned.[9]

There can be no doubt as to what we are to understand. The circuitous logic of the argument was, of course, not recognized as such in the light of the authority of the early church, which authority had to be maintained in order to combat the heresies which continued to spring up.

We may now turn to St. Augustine's conception of the teaching-learning situation. Early in the *De Doctrina Christiana* St. Augustine defines charity as the love of God and insists that charity and humility must be brought by the student to his investigation of Scripture if he is to gain from it the truth which is there. He then discusses as prerequisite to the study of Scripture basic knowledge in such fields as languages, grammar, numbers, and music: language as an aid in choosing between translations, grammar as an aid in ferreting out the sense of passages which have perhaps been poorly organized or punctuated, numbers as an aid in understanding certain mysterious significances involving number symbolism, and music as an aid to, among other things, an understanding of the significance of rhythmic structure. Of particular sig-

[9] Saint Augustine, *On Christian Doctrine*, trans. D. W. Robertson, Jr. (New York, 1958), p. 7.

nificance to the learning situation is the lengthy discussion in the *De Magistro* of the efficacy of words in the teacher-pupil relationship, but this will be discussed in another connection.

In order to further discuss St. Augustine's influence on early medieval literary tradition it is necessary to investigate a fundamental duality which appears to be a basic assumption in his thought. To St. Augustine the problems involved in Christian instruction and in literary theory are the same since to him literature means, primarily, Holy Scripture and all writing is part of the teaching process. The opening statement of the *De Doctrina Christiana*, cited above, sets up the entire treatise around the two complementary elements of learning and teaching. His conception of man's primary relationship to physical creation turns on a duality just as fundamental:

> 3. Some things are to be enjoyed, others to be used, and there are others which are to be enjoyed and used. Those things which are to be enjoyed make us blessed. Those things which are to be used help and, as it were, sustain us as we move toward blessedness in order that we may gain and cling to those things which make us blessed.[10]

The fundamental duality is, of course, that between things to be used and things to be enjoyed. The state in which man can both use and enjoy a thing, in which there is a reconciliation of the two opposing and complementary aspects of our participation in God's creation, is the state which man should constantly seek. In such a state he is fulfilling God's will by both loving the thing as part of God's revealed love for mankind and using it as a means of enlarging his awareness of God's love and eventually his awareness of God Himself. St. Augustine goes on to say in the same passage that should we begin to enjoy a thing so that we cling to it with affection for its own sake we impede our *use* of it for the ends of higher enjoyment. That which is alone to be enjoyed is God. The neo-Platonism in the notion is obvious. There are other aspects of this duality just as fundamental to St. Augustine's theory. When he speaks of the proper attitude in which one should approach the study of Scripture he speaks of love of self (lust) as opposed to love of God (charity), when he speaks of language he

[10] Saint Augustine, *On Christian Doctrine*, p. 9.

speaks of it as either literal or figurative, when he speaks of rhetoric he speaks of eloquence as opposed to fact (truth), when he speaks of words he speaks of signs as opposed to things, and when he speaks of study he speaks of love of knowledge (superficial fact) as opposed to love of truth.

Of fundamental importance to this whole consideration is the means of distinguishing between language which is literal and language which is figurative. At one point, discussing literal language, St. Augustine says:

17. Therefore, whatever is read in the Scriptures concerning bitterness or anger in the words or deeds of the person of God or of his saints is of value for the destruction of the reign of cupidity. If it is obviously so intended it is not to be referred to something else as though it were figurative.[11]

Concerning figurative language, he says:

18. Those things which seem almost shameful to the inexperienced, whether simply spoken or actually performed either by the person of God or by men whose sanctity is commended to us, all are figurative, and their secrets are to be removed as kernels from the husk as nourishment for charity . . . .
19. Careful attention is therefore to be paid to what is proper to places, times and persons lest we condemn the shameful too hastily.[12]

At another point he says:

24. If a locution is admonitory, condemning either vice or crime or commending either utility or beneficence, it is not figurative. But if it seems to commend either vice or crime or to condemn either utility or beneficence, it is figurative.[13]

Such dogmatic insistence upon the one unchangeable truth which is to be sought in the Scriptures and on the duty of the student to find that truth leads us to a further question, that concerning the nature of figurative or symbolic language as it was thought of in medieval literary theory.

We have already commented on the medieval notion that in every human experience the just and benevolent guiding hand of

[11] Saint Augustine, *On Christian Doctrine*, p. 89.
[12] Saint Augustine, *On Christian Doctrine*, pp. 90-91.
[13] Saint Augustine, *On Christian Doctrine*, p. 93.

God can be seen. No human experience, of whatever nature or however slight, could be without religious, that is to say, symbolic significance. It would follow, since created nature is an integral part of all human experience, that a man of the Middle Ages would likely not have taken pleasure in anything for its own sake any more than he would have read the Bible simply to enjoy the literal story or its style. The recognition of this rigorous conditioning does not, however, answer the question at hand – that as to the nature of the language as such.

Symbolism in the Middle Ages was much more likely to be considered a condition of the created universe than a matter of style or rhetoric, as it is in the twentieth century. To be sure, there was emphasis on rhetoric in teaching but the emphasis was more sophistical than philosophical, more a matter of effectiveness and persuasion than of the essential condition of things. In modern theory we set up a category which perhaps slightly overlaps with but excludes the symbolic from, say, the realistic or the naturalistic or the allegorical. Such a separation of views found no place in medieval thought. All writing, since it dealt with human experience, was considered necessarily symbolic; the words as signs of the created things or of man's discernment of them. If this be so, we have returned to the center of St. Augustine's theory of language and to his doctrine of the polarity of enjoyment and use. Since words, that is, language, are only means of cognition or conveying of ideas (teaching), it must be the duty of the student and teacher to find the proper relationship existing between words and cognition and things cognized and thereby to make clear the true nature of the universe and of man's experience of it. Language cannot be other than symbolic.

A second aspect of medieval language theory is that symbolism to the medieval mind was much more nearly related to allegory than is so to the modern mind. The nature of Dante's symbolism is a case in point. The term 'symbolic allegory' has to be used in order properly to deal with *The Divine Comedy*. It is apparent that St. Augustine held the same conception of symbolism and that language, cognition, and things cognized were to him all levels of a complex structure (creation), which was essentially a symbolic allegory of God's love. It is this conception of the nature of things which leads St. Augustine to his theory of language and of teaching and writing. Taken together with the insistence that dogma is to be equated with truth, the theory necessarily resulted in much distortion of secular literature in particular, as the devout clergy did their best to wrest from the ancient writings interpretations in line with theological doctrine. Distortion is evident as well in the tradition of biblical exegesis. Such distortion was the inevitable result of the method, but it is the method, not the distortion, that is important to this discussion, for the method began inevitably to influence the writing of Christian literature as well as the interpretation of it. Bernard Huppé sums up the effect of the influence of the method as follows:

> The Christian theory of interpretive reading made possible the preservation of pagan letters, for the Christian could see in Vergil's poetic mastery the sign, not of the devil's charm, but of God's eloquence. In truth, the Christian felt that he alone could understand what Vergil was inspired to relate and prophesy; by interpreting it in the light of revelation, the Christian could restore Vergil's poetry to its Master.... This method involved a systematic Christianizing of pagan myths and fables by interpreting them as allegories in the light of Christian revelation.... The Christian understanding of the Bible and of pagan literature made almost inevitable the development of a theory that serious poetry should be allusive, enigmatic, periphrastic.[14]

The notion that serious poetry should be enigmatic leads us into one further point of the discussion of medieval literary theory which has been mentioned but which has not been commented on specifically – eloquence of style. It was noted in the discussion of the fundamental duality underlying the allegorical interpretation of literature that eloquence is opposed in St. Augustine's system to fact or truth. Eloquence, however, was acceptable and under certain circumstances even desirable. In Book IV of the *De Doctrina Christiana* St. Augustine makes a lengthy and thorough distinction between the emptiness of the eloquence of the rhetoricians or the pagan writers and the strength of the eloquence of the writers of Holy Scripture. What he says at this point is primarily concerned with oratory but his treatment of the various figures of speech is

---

[14] Bernard F. Huppé, *Doctrine and Poetry* (New York, 1959), pp. 29-30.

equally applicable to the study of written literature. What St. Augustine sees as emptiness in the eloquence of the pagan writings or in the work of the rhetoricians is, of course, their lack of concern with the revealed truth of Scripture. These writings may follow meticulously the complex rules of the art of rhetoric and in so doing achieve an easy sweetness of style, but the sweetness of style (eloquence) is empty because it is interested in itself alone. This is his distinction between the enjoyment and the use of a thing. In fact, he suggests that true eloquence can better be learned, not from a careful study of the rules of rhetoric alone, but rather from a study of the writings of truly eloquent men.

> ... those with acute and eager minds more readily learn eloquence by reading and hearing the eloquent than by following the rules of eloquence. There is no lack of ecclesiastical literature, including that outside of the canon established in a place of secure authority, which, if read by a capable man, even though he is interested more in what is said than in the eloquence with which it is said, will imbue him with that eloquence while he is studying. [15]

He further suggests in the same passage that in order to develop this eloquence to the fullest one should join to his reading practice in "writing, dictating, or speaking what he has learned according to the rule of piety and faith", a statement important to the future of poetic theory in the Middle Ages. The truly strong eloquence results from a devout application to the study of the revealed truth of Scripture; it grows naturally, St. Augustine implies, with the student's involvement in the task of expressing as forcefully as possible the divine significance of the Scriptures. Granted the acceptable nature of this strong eloquence, plus the fact that he says elsewhere in the *De Doctrina Christiana* that

> ... the obscurity itself of the divine and wholesome writings was a part of a kind of eloquence through which our understandings should be benefited not only by the discovery of what lies hidden but also by exercise.[16]

it is possible to see more clearly why the tradition of "allusive, enigmatic, periphrastic" serious poetry grew during the early Middle

[15] Saint Augustine, *On Christian Doctrine*, p. 119.
[16] Saint Augustine, *On Christian Doctrine*, p. 123.

Ages. The ideas expressed by St. Augustine were not new, but his bringing them together, applying them directly to the problem of Christian instruction, and stating them so forcefully gave them new life and spread them abroad over the Christian world as the accepted methods of Christian education.

The principles of interpretive reading and its corollary, the tradition of symbolic or allegorical composition, eventually dominated all medieval literary theory and may be traced through the Carolingian Renaissance up into the fifteenth century.[17] The method had begun in Alexandria, been introduced into Africa by St. Augustine, had been carried via Marseilles into France by St. Martin of Tours, into England by St. Augustine of Canterbury, and eventually back to the continent again by Alcuin when he went to establish the court schools for Charlemagne. From the early sixth century on, the method was an influence in the schools which were founded in England under the banner of Rome, and after the synod of Whitby the way was clear to introduce it into the establishments which theretofore had been under Irish rule. It seems reasonable to assume that, under the influence of these Augustinian principles, English churchmen might well have begun quite early the process of turning over in their minds the Germanic legends as sung by the *scops* in order to find in them whatever of God's truth and solid eloquence they could convert to Christian use. Possibly they began also, as St. Augustine had suggested, to give written expression to Christian concepts, using the material of the Germanic culture into which they had moved. What better way to reach the unlearned masses than through their own songs – altered and reemphasized in order to gain allegorical overtones. The fact that Christian lore appears in the earliest of the Old English poems, *Widsith* (c. 650), is significant of the fact that the English churchmen had begun the attempt to work Christian themes into the

---

[17] Citations to substantiate this statement would be too numerous for inclusion in a footnote. Attention may be called to the moral implications of the *solaas-sentence* dichotomy and specially to the complex philosophical implications of the concept of sign as thing (word or object). Involvement with these problems may be traced from Isidore of Seville through Hugh of St. Victor, John of Salisbury, to Chaucer, and on into the fourteenth century in Thomas Usk's preface to his *Testament of Love*.

material. That they did this should not seem surprising for yet another reason. During the early stages of the conversion they had difficulty in keeping some of the invaders, once converted, from slipping back into their pagan practices. The seventh-century missionaries in England were meeting their problems in much the same way that Origen had met similar problems among heretics of the Middle East about the middle of the third century. These heretics believed that they had found scriptural evidence to support the idea that the soul existed in the blood and hence ceased to exist with physical death. Origen answered their doubts by interpreting the body allegorically as spirit – the eyes and ears signifying understanding, etc. He pointed to texts which substantiated his interpretation, centering on Genesis 9:5, "of the blood of your souls account will be asked". Here, he said, was proof that when Scripture mentioned blood it was to be interpreted allegorically as spirit, not to be taken literally as the blood of the body. Beryl Smalley in commenting on the episode says,

The actuality of the scene forbids us to think of allegory as an artifice, imposed on Scripture by philosophers who were "out of touch with the masses". Rather it was a necessary condition of the spread of Christianity among the people.[18]

The statement applies with equal validity to the situation of the missionaries among the Germanic people in seventh-century England. In this connection one might recall Alcuin's remark in one of his letters that Bede presented his message to the people "in simple language but in subtle sense".

During the nineteenth century certain German scholars, attempting to explain the presence of the Christian elements, propounded the so-called interpolation theory, their idea being that some pious monk or monks had simply taken works from the Germanic oral tradition and had interlarded them with bits of Christian lore. In this way they accounted not only for the Christian elements but also for what they felt was crudeness and lack of artistic unity in the poems. It seems, however, that much more than mere interpolation was effected by the monks who worked over the pagan

[18] Beryl Smalley, *The Study of the Bible in the Middle Ages* (New York, 1952), p. 11.

material, that they, in fact, rewrote and conceptually reformed the material they found into poems of a definite Christian nature. Further, it seems to me that the early scholars in Old English, both in the United States and Europe, were too quick to explain away difficulties as crudities in the poetry, and that their followers have been too quick to repeat the evaluations of their forerunners without sufficient close study of the poems in terms of theme and structure.

2. GROWTH OF THE SCHOOLS

The transmission of the great tradition of patristic scholarship and exegesis stemming from the work of St. Augustine could have been effected only through the monastic centers. Since it is the purpose of this study to show the growth and continuity of the patristic traditions of interpretation and teaching in the monasteries of the Old English period, it is necessary to show briefly the existence of books and libraries in both Ireland and England early enough to have allowed the tradition to affect the writing of Old English poetry. Perhaps the earliest evidence for the presence of books in the islands is in connection with the ministry of St. Patrick. There is some reason to believe that Pope Sixtus gave him books to take with him to Ireland and that later he himself went to Rome and brought more books to Armagh. There is further evidence that he gave parts of copies of Holy Scripture to certain Irish chieftains and that he had books at Tara.[19] Stokes, in the *Tripartite Life*, reports that St. Patrick customarily gave boys, brought to him for acceptance into the monastic establishments, an alphabet along with the sacrament of baptism. It is well known that Patrick himself was not a formally educated man and that in his *Confession* he laments his lack of learning. He was, however, a great missionary and under the aegis of his work the tradition of the learned ministry got its start in Ireland. The copying of manuscripts, probably circulated from Gaul, began early in Patrick's ministry. We should also point to the learning of such men as Columban

[19] Ernest A. Savage, *Old English Literature* (Chicago, 1912), p. 4.

(d. 615), whose monasteries at Luxeuil, Bobbio, and St. Gall became homes of some of the world's greatest libraries and where provisions were made for "teaching in schools, copying manuscripts, and for daily reading". St. Columba of Iona (d. 597) was a lover of books and learning. In fact, legend records his having left Ireland as the result of an argument with his old teacher Finnian of Moville over a book. He had books at his monastery on Iona, which became a center of learning in Scotland. From the sixth to the eighth centuries Ireland was an outstanding center of learning, drawing many students from Wales and England, and in return strengthening the growth of monastic schools in both these countries. Although the Romano-British and Irish churches were in the beginning different in structure, by the time of St. Augustine of Canterbury they apparently followed essentially the same forms of worship. It would certainly be reasonable to assume that the great strength of the Irish church, particularly after it was cut off from the continent by the Germanic invasions of England, pulled the British church, after its retreat into Wales, into line with Irish practices.

An important aspect of the influence of the Irish schools upon the development of the Old English poetic tradition is the fact that the Irish schools preserved a study of secular letters during the years in which such study was being strongly opposed on the continent by the Roman church. The maintenance of secular studies is another result of the virtual isolation of the Irish church after the Germanic invasions of England. The amount of knowledge of classical languages is debatable, but there is evidence for believing that both Columban and Secundinus knew Latin and Greek. At any rate, secular learning was brought to the Anglo-Saxon nations by the Irish long before the founding of the school at Canterbury in 669 by Theodore and Hadrian.[20] How much knowledge of the continental Christian Latin writers the Irish schools had is not

[20] Possible influence of the classical epic in *Beowulf* has been studied, see, for instance, Albert S. Cook, "Greek Parallels to Certain Features of the *Beowulf*", *PQ*, V (1926), 226-234 and Tom Burns Haber, *A Comparative Study of the Beowulf and the Aeneid* (Princeton, 1931). One ready source of such knowledge of the classics to the Old English poets might have been the Irish schools.

accurately ascertainable, but we are fairly certain from evidence presented above that St. Patrick took books with him and that there was fairly widespread copying of manuscripts; we must assume, it seems to me, some knowledge in Ireland of the continental Latin tradition in addition to the highly important knowledge of secular letters. There can be no doubt that the *peregrini* from the Irish monasteries who brought learning to Scotland and England in the sixth century had behind them and brought with them a wide knowledge of both secular and sacred writing. The evidence for continuing Christian influence on English culture is strengthened even more if we accept the strong possibility of the existence of the church and monastic centers in Wales during the period of the invasions.

Of primary importance is the evidence for the existence of libraries and schools within the immediate area of England. The importance of the English schools is different from that of the Irish schools, although both are important to the development of the Old English poetic tradition. The difference in the influence of the two is that in the English monastic schools we can discern the definite presence of Augustinian theories concerning study and teaching, while it is the Irish monasteries with their *peregrini* which give to Old English poetry much of its elegiac quality and its theme of the lonely exile. The Irish influence is more of a pervading atmosphere while the native English influence gave it its didactic cast. This is, of course, an oversimplification, but the lines, I think, are generally true.

We have what seems to be the irrefutable authority of Bede for St. Augustine of Canterbury's possession of books when he arrived in England, books given him by Pope Gregory. Bede records that Gregory sent to St. Augustine in order to aid him in his work

... several fellow laborers and ministers of the word ... sacred vessels and vestments for the altars, also ornaments for the churches, and vestments for the priests and clerks, as likewise relics of the Holy apostles and martyrs; besides many books.[21]

---

[21]   Bede, *Ecclesiastical History*, I, xxix. All references are to the translation of J. Stevens (1723), rev. J. A. Giles (London, Everyman Library, 1910).

Bede also records that St. Augustine and his fellow monks began to teach soon after their arrival, receiving from those they taught (*quos docebant*) only the food necessary to their existence. Just how the verb *docebant* is to be construed is questionable. It may signify no more than the preaching to the multitudes who flocked to hear about the new religion; it may, however, mean that St. Augustine and his helpers had actually set up a small-scale school and had begun to teach. If so, a school existed at Canterbury about 70 years before the arrival of Theodore and Hadrian and may have served as a foundation for the one they set up. Since it is definitely known that Gregory was a close follower of the Augustinian theories of interpretive reading and exegesis and of the Benedictine Rule with its emphasis on *lectio divina*, it seems reasonable to assume that the books he sent would have contained biblical commentary, saints' lives, and other works of a similar nature, in addition to the Scriptures, the kinds of books necessary to the establishment of a small episcopal school. We can be certain, however, that Gregory would not have sent any books containing secular writings. English students at this period would have gained their only exposure to secular knowledge through the Irish schools.

King Sigebert of East Anglia, whom Bede describes as "a most Christian and learned man", is thought to have established a monastic school in East Anglia about 631, although there is no conclusive evidence. Sigebert had spent three years in exile in Gaul during the reign of his brother Eorpwald and had received baptism while in exile. It is thought that he was exposed to the monastic school system in Gaul and brought the idea back to East Anglia with him.

It is fairly certain that at about the same time that Sigebert is supposed to have established his school the Irish monk-teacher Maildulf founded the monastery school at Malmesbury. It was this school to which Aldhelm first went and to which he eventually returned as abbot in 675. The foundation of an Irish school in this southern part of the island enhances the claims for the strength of the Irish influence in England, particularly in view of the fact that the establishment at Glastonbury is almost certainly Irish and of an earlier date than Malmesbury.

Also at about this same time, about 635, the most important monastery in Northumbria was being founded on Lindisfarne Island by Aidan, the great Irish bishop. This monastery with its library became the most influential center of Irish Christianity on the island for many years. Its monks produced, about 700, one of the greatest religious and art treasures of the Christian era, the Lindisfarne Gospels, written in the beautiful round hand. Some of the greatest of the Irish abbots and bishops held their seats of authority there, such men as Aidan, Colman, Eata, and the famous St. Cuthbert (d. 687) who finally won the majority of the monks over to the Roman rule.

As early as 625 Paulinus, sent north by St. Augustine from Canterbury earlier in the century to preach among the Northumbrians, was named archbishop of York, and in 627 King Edwin of Northumbria built the first minster there. This was the beginning of the establishment which was by the middle of the eighth century to boast one of the great libraries of the western world. It was here that Alcuin became librarian and schoolmaster in 776. His description of the school and its masters and of the library holdings of the school is among the most important documents in the history of the church and of education in England.

The double monastery at Whitby under Abbess Hilda was, according to Bede, established in 656. This was one of the monasteries in which both monks and nuns were housed. Another of the double monasteries which was well known throughout the island was that at Barking, founded by Erkenwald, bishop of London, in 670. We know that there must have been a library at Whitby, for Bede's story of Caedmon, the first poet in English whose name is definitely known, tells us that the morning after Caedmon had miraculously composed his hymn he was taken by the steward to the abbess, who ordered him "in the presence of many learned men" to tell his dream and repeat the verses. Further, Bede tells us that Abbess Hilda, having heard the decision of the learned men that Caedmon had had heavenly grace conferred upon him,

... instructed him to quit the secular habit, and take upon him the monastic life, which being accordingly done, she associated him to the rest of her brethren in the monastery, and ordered that he should be taught the whole series of sacred history.[22]

It seems certain that in order to teach Caedmon "the whole series of sacred history" the monks must have had at their disposal a library of some size.

Between the years of 665 and 690 the two famous monasteries of Wearmouth and Jarrow were being built and supplied with books by Benedit Bishop, who made three trips to Rome between 663 and 690 in order to bring books back to England. Wearmouth was founded first, in 675, and Jarrow followed in 682. These libraries, together with those at Lindisfarne and York, remained the center of learning of the western world until the Danish marauders burned them to the ground, Lindisfarne in 793 and Jarrow in 794. Only York temporarily survived the holocaust, and England's supremacy in the worlds of both secular and Christian learning was brought crashing to earth. Not again until during the reign of King Alfred the Great (d. 901), almost a century later, did learning begin to have a revival in the island. It was at the school of Wearmouth and Jarrow, since the twin monasteries of SS. Peter and Paul were meant to be one establishment, that Bede spent his life, eventually becoming master of the school. These monasteries were set up according to the rule of Rome rather than of the Irish church.

England's most famous school was established at Canterbury in 669 by the new archbishop, Theodore of Tarsus, and his assistant, the abbot Hadrian. Theodore was a native of Tarsus, the home of St. Paul, and had studied at Athens. He was proficient in both Latin and Greek. Abbot Hadrian from Africa, and a monk at the Niridane monastery near Naples, also knew both Latin and Greek. In fact, he probably spoke Greek fluently, since it was at that time still widely used as the vernacular in the towns of southern Italy. These two men brought with them many books which they added to the collection begun by St. Augustine and soon spread the fame of their teaching throughout the island to such an extent that they began to attract students away from the Irish schools. For the first time, an English school began to overshadow the great schools in

[22] Bede, IV, xxiv.

Ireland. Bede records the phenomenal success of the two great teachers:

And foreasmuch as both of them were, as has been said before, well read both in sacred and secular literature, they gathered a crowd of disciples, and there daily flowed from them rivers of knowledge to water the hearts of their hearers; and, together with the books of holy writ, they also taught them the arts of ecclesiastical poetry, astronomy, and arithmetic. A testimony of which is, that there are still living at this day some of their scholars, who are as well versed in the Greek and Latin tongues as in their own, in which they were born.[23]

Bede was writing this about 730, not more than half a century after the founding of the school, a fact which attests the effectiveness of the teaching there.

These are only the most famous of the monastic schools and libraries in England during the seventh and eighth centuries. There were many others. It should be pointed out that most of the schools were, in their monastic rule, either already Roman or were being gradually won over to the Roman rule following the Synod of Whitby. The Irish influence, however, did not die out immediately. In fact, it has been pointed out that there was a married clergyman in Hexham as late as the early twelfth century, a practice definitely Irish rather than Roman. Be this as it may, the Roman church was gaining the ultimate control, and, with the Roman church came the Benedictine Rule and the Augustinian theories of study and teaching. Although the patristic tradition proper is said to have died with Bede, the influence of the Augustinian teaching certainly remained, perpetuated in England by the Benedictine houses and throughout the continent by the Carolingian Renaissance to which Alcuin carried in 781 the great wealth of Anglo-Saxon and Irish Christian tradition. Perhaps of even more importance to the discussion is the fact that these schools existed with their great wealth of learning and scholarship even before the first of the poems in Old English were written and continued to flourish throughout the most vital years of the life of that tradition. The presence of Christian material in all of the poems has never

[23]   Bede, IV, ii.

been denied. Therefore, it does not seem unreasonable to assume that they were written in or under the direction of the monastic centers or episcopal schools, for the purpose of converting the pagan popular oral tradition into a vehicle for the propagation of the Christian faith. This method of spreading the word of the Scriptures had been in use for at least three centuries, as we can see from the attitudes of St. Jerome and particularly of St. Augustine toward the proper use of pagan material.

3. LITERARY GENRES

In the early centuries of the Christian era the church fathers won a signal victory over pagan literature: they converted most of it to Christian didactic use by finding in it unsuspected intimations of divine truth. The allegorical method of interpretive reading is at the heart of this reconciliation of pagan and Christian cultures. The fact that the earliest Christian writing was done by apologists made it unavoidable that such writing bear the didactic stamp, but it was St. Augustine, nearly two centuries later, who stated the principles as a method. What is of interest is the form which this didacticism took. As the body of literature grew and writers of great talent began to make their appearances here and there, it was inevitable that new ways of presenting the Christian story would make their appearance. These same types of Christian literature written from the third to the sixth centuries on the continent appear in the Old English tradition of the seventh, eighth, and ninth centuries. Further, it can be shown that in most cases the Latin authors of the continent were well known in the schools in which, in all probability, the Old English poems were written.

In moving to an examination of genres we must take note of a large and important step in the development of the allegorical tradition. Up to this point we have been discussing the patristic and exegetical traditions, which limit themselves exclusively to explication of passages of Scripture or to, in the period which we are considering, defense of doctrinal decrees. When we move to the study of genres we move into the entirely new realm of imaginative creation. The subject matter of the creative effort may be the same as that of the exegetical and patristic traditions but the method, nay, the entire mode, is different. To be sure, it can be argued that the Scriptures themselves are the works of men, but no serious student of the Middle Ages would have dared entertain such an idea, but would have assumed a divine source of inspiration in the Scriptures as opposed to the mortal source of inspiration in the work of the poets. Such an assumption made necessary the methods of study and teaching as stated by St. Augustine. However, since these methods were applied to the study of all acceptable literature, they would naturally find application in original composition, particularly that which used biblical material and Christian legend as subject matter.

The literary types which we find in continental Christian Latin writing and which recur in Old English are the Christian allegory, the Christian epic, the saint's life, Old and New Testament paraphrase, Christian lyric, and Christian elegy.

Christian allegory is perhaps the first of the genres to make its appearance, in the poem *Phoenix*, attributed to Lactantius and written about the first quarter of the fourth century. F. J. E. Raby thinks Prudentius' *Psychomachia* is the earliest Christian allegory, while E. K. Rand calls it the first Christian allegorical epic. There is no way, of course, to reconcile disagreements over details of dating and genre of the early literature, and perhaps no need.

The *Psychomachia* consists of a series of epic combats between personified virtues and vices, the kind of allegorizing which was to become so popular later in medieval poetry and drama: Faith overcomes Worship-of-the-old-Gods; Chastity defeats Lust the Sodomite; Long-Suffering proves Wrath's Nemesis when Wrath at last, unable to discompose her enemy, turns her shaft in rage into her own breast; Lowliness, aided unknowingly by Deceit, is saved from Pride. It is interesting to note in the section of the poem dealing with chastity a reference to the Old Testament story of Judith, which reference brings up the possibility of allegorical overtones in the Old English poem *Judith*. There is in the work of Prudentius (d. c. 410) another possibility of allegorical interpretation, in the series of hymns called *Cathemerinon* [The Daily

Round]. Examples from three of the hymns will show the thin line between allegory and symbol in the work. In the first hymn, "Hymnus ad Galli Cantum" [A Hymn for Cock-Crow], the opening quatrain states the symbolism of the Cock as Christ:

> Ales diei nuntius
> lucem propinquam praecinit;
> nos excitator mentium
> iam Christus ad vitam vocat.

'The bird that heralds the day forewarns that dawn is at hand; now Christ, the awakener of our souls, calls us to life.'[24]

The opening quatrain of the second hymn, "Hymnus Matutinus" [A Morning Hymn], states the symbolism of darkness as disorder and of the dawn's light as Christ:

> Nox et tenebrae et nubila,
> confusa mundi et turbida,
> lux intrat, albescit polus,
> Christus venit, discedite.

'Night and darkness and clouds, all the world's perplexed disorder, get ye gone! The dawn comes in, the sky is lightening, Christ is coming.'

In Hymn No. 5, "Hymnus ad Incensum Lucernae" [A Hymn for the Lighting of the Lamp], the symbolism is a little more drawn out but just as clear once it develops:

> Inventor rutili, dux bone, luminis,
> qui certis vicibus tempera dividis,
> merso sole chaos ingruit horridum.
> lucem redde tuis, Christe, fidelibus.
>   quamvis innumero sidere regiam
> lunarique polum lampade pinxeris,
> incussu silicis lumina nos tamen
> monstras saxigeno semine quaerere,
>   ne nesciret homo spem sibi luminis
> in Christi solido corpore conditam,
> qui dici stabilem se voluit petram,
> nostris igniculis unde genus venit.

[24] H. J. Thomson (ed.), *Prudentius*, 2 vols. (Cambridge, 1949), I, 6. Hereinafter cited as Thomson.

'Creator of the glowing light, our kindly guide, who dost divide the times in a fixed order of seasons, now the sun has sunk and the gruesome darkness comes upon us; give light again, O Christ, to Thy faithful ones. Albeit Thou hast adorned the heavens, Thy royal court, with countless stars and with the moon's lamp, yet Thou teachest us to seek light from a stone-born spark by striking the flint, that man might know that his hope of light is founded on the firm body of Christ, who willed that He be called the steadfast rock, from whence our little fires draw their origin.'

Obviously we are dealing here with symbols, but with symbols bearing a relationship with reality so close to the one-to-one ratio of allegory that to draw a distinction between the two is difficult.

The final example of Christian allegory we will deal with is the poem *De Pascha*, attributed to Marius Victorinus (b. c. 300), perhaps the same Victorinus, the African philosopher and rhetorician, whose conversion is related by St. Augustine in his *Confessions*. The poem is an allegorical treatment of the Cross. The early preoccupation with the Cross points ahead to the use of the same theme in two outstanding examples of Old English poetry, *The Dream of the Rood* and *Elene*.

Another of the genres which appears in the early continental Christian Latin writers is the Christian epic, a form extremely popular in the Old English tradition as well, as exemplified by such works as *Andreas, Elene*, the fragmentary *Fight at Finnesburg* and *Waldere*, not to mention *Beowulf*. There are also definite heroic qualities in *Judith*. The earliest known example of the Christian epic is Juvencus' *Evangeliorum Libri IV*, written c. 330. The poem is a heroic treatment of the Gospels, the division into four books being symbolic of the four Gospels. The poem appears to be based on St. Matthew and to weave in episodes from the other Gospels. One of the most interesting things about the technique of Juvencus in the poem is his use of epithets; God, for instance, becomes the High-Thunderer and the Lofty Throned Parent. The Homeric epithet is in the background of such a technique, and one is led to wonder if its transmission in the Juvencus may possibly contain any influence on the development of the Old English kenning.

Four poets of fifth-century Gaul made the inevitable return to the Old Testament in search of epic material: Cyprian with his *Heptateuches* (a fragment), Hilary of Arles with his versification of the book of Genesis (c. 429), Marius Victor with a paraphrase of the book of Genesis, and Avitus, bishop of Vienne, with five books in classical heroic meter dealing with, in turn, the creation, original sin, the judgment of God, the Flood, and the Crossing of the Red Sea. Avitus' description of paradise is perhaps reminiscent of passages from the *Phoenix*, both in Latin and in Old English.

Sedulius, about the middle of the fifth century, did an epic treatment which bridged the Old and the New Testaments, the *Carmen Paschale*. By emphasizing the miraculous happenings in both Testaments, Sedulius succeeded in effecting a smooth transition from one to the other while at the same time keeping the Gospel story as his center of interest. He accomplishes this transition by using the Old Testament miracles not only to show the power of God in the world but also to prophesy the coming of Jesus. The interpretation of the Old Testament as prophetic of the New was one of the most important aspects of the interpretive method and influenced heavily the composition of Christian poetry both on the continent and in England. The application of the method to poetry is closely allied with the typological tradition in exegesis, again exemplifying the relationship between the traditions of biblical commentary and poetic composition in the early Middle Ages. After the first book, which is taken up with the Old Testament miracles, the rest of the work goes on to the miracles of Jesus and to the resurrection and ascension. There is a great deal of Christian allegory and symbolism, such as having the three gifts of the magi parallel the three persons of the Godhead and, further, represent the three aspects of time involved in the infinite: past, present, and future.

In the sixth century Arator took a new subject as material for epic treatment, the Acts of the Apostles. The poem contains several elements of mysticism and allegory which made it highly popular during the Middle Ages. Finally, a certain heroic note is to be noticed in Prudentius' *Peristephanon*. The individual pieces in this work certainly cannot be called epic but that they have the heroic mood, which is one of the major aspects of the epic, should be noted. Prudentius' martyrs are undaunted by their suffering; they always have the last word, extolling the virtues of martyrdom and reducing to a kind of grim absurdity the tortures inflicted upon them by the powerless heathen. To be sure, their power is always their faith in the presence of Christ, which fact gives their heroism its distinctly Christian character.

The saint's life was a popular literary genre among the continental Christian Latin writers, as it was also to be among the Old English. Damasus, who became bishop of Rome in 366, gives us the earliest example of the type of work which was to develop into the full treatment of the life, sufferings, and miracles of the saint. His work was made up entirely of epigrams and inscriptions which he wrote to commemorate the tombs of the martyrs, to the discovery of which he devoted a great deal of his life. Although the limits of the limitations of the inscription did not allow much room for elaboration, he became the first poet to celebrate the sufferings of the martyrs. A contemporary of Damasus, Paulinus of Nola (355-431) added to the development of the genre with a number of short poems praising saints and martyrs. Prudentius in his *Peristephanon* carried the celebration of the suffering and the miraculous delivery of the martyrs a step farther toward the full development of the form. In these 14 poems, which range in length from 18 to 1140 lines, Prudentius vividly details the trials of the martyr-saints. It was left for the late fifth-century poet Paulinus of Perigueux, however, to write the full-fledged saint's life. At the request of Perpetuus, bishop of Tours from 458-88, he composed an account of more than 3000 lines of the life of St. Martin of Tours. In the development of this particular genre we probably have the outward signs of the growth of the cult of the martyrs, which was to become so marked a characteristic of the medieval church. By the time the church had reached England, a century after the writing of Paulinus of Perigueux, the cult had had time to gain in strength and popularity, so that in Old English poetry we get some of the outstanding examples of the genre in western literature, typified by *Andreas, Juliana, Elene,* and *Guthlac.*

In dealing with the saint's life and other Christian material in

Old English poetry, scholars have always commented on the presence of the heroic and epic modes without ever satisfactorily explaining their presence. They have usually attributed the modes, particularly in the saint's life, to the fact that the poems are written in the tradition of the *scop* and make use of Germanic heroic and comitatus formulae from the oral tradition. In this way many have been able to account for what they call the essentially heathen nature of the treatment of Christian material. It is usual to say, for instance, that Andreas is presented as a comitatus warrior surrounded by traditional images of Germanic battle poetry and sea imagery. We find the same statements concerning other poems, such as *Elene*, some of the language of *Juliana* and *Guthlac*, and passages of *Christ*. It would seem that scholars have overlooked the influence of the Old Testament in these poems. They have seen the Old Testament simply as a source for epic material which pleased a warrior-like audience of Germanic tribesmen, but this is not going far enough. We have pointed to the presence of the Old Testament tradition with its epic atmosphere among continental writers and to the exegetical tradition which Christianized this material. If Old English poetry is a part of the whole continental literary tradition, and evidence that it is seems overwhelming, it seems reasonable to assume that Old Testament tradition supplied a large part of the epic atmosphere in which the saints' lives were composed both on the continent and in England. To be sure, traditional Germanic images appear, but to point to them exclusively and argue on the basis of their presence for a purely Germanic and therefore heathen atmosphere in the treatment is to overlook the essentially Christian heritage of the development. The same argument may be mounted against such statements as that of Ellen Elizabeth Wardale in her *Chapters on Old English Literature* that *Exodus*, although written by a churchman, is entirely free of Christian influence, that its atmosphere is essentially pre-Christian.[25] Such an attitude seems to me a part of the scholarly tradition which explained the battle and sea imagery in Old English poetry by saying that the Old English were warlike and loved the sea,

[25] Ellen Elizabeth Wardale, *Chapters on Old English Literature* (London, 1939), p. 129.

statements which, of course, explain nothing and which dismiss the poetry and its literary tradition from consideration.

The tradition of Old and New Testament paraphrase has been covered already in the section on the Christian epic, since the two genres are for the most part inseparable. Two anonymous poems and the work of two well known poets remain to be mentioned in connection with the paraphrase tradition. From about the third or fourth century come two poems based on Old Testament story: *De Sodoma* and *De Iona*. The first, of course, relates the destruction of Sodom and the story of Lot and his wife. The second poem, a fragment probably by the same author, gives the story of Jonah up to the time of his being swallowed by the fish. The latter poem states directly its application as an allegory of the Resurrection. Here is another example of the Christianizing of Old Testament material. We shall see the same allegorical development in a study of *Exodus*. Paulinus of Nola, about the beginning of the fifth century, did three paraphrases from the Psalter, and Dracontius in Africa, in the last quarter of the fifth century, did a long didactic paraphrase covering the incidents in both the Old and New Testaments, but centering almost exclusively on the Old Testament, where the poet appears to be more at home. The term 'paraphrase' does not really describe the technique of these poets, since their purpose was apparently, in line with exegetical tradition, to bring the Old and the New Testaments into line with each other in order to show the development of the one into the other without significant break or alteration of essential truths.

Elegiac, mystic, and lyric qualities were to be somewhat later developments in Christian literature. Paulinus of Nola wrote what is recognized as the first fully developed Christian elegy, a poem on the death of a boy named Celsus. The poem is perhaps the earliest example of the consolation theme which we find more fully developed in the Old English Christian elegies *The Wanderer* and *The Seafarer*. There are also lyric passages in Prudentius' *Peristephanon,* such as the following in the closing lines of the hymn to Eulalia:

> carpite purpureas violas
> sanguineosque crocos metite.

non caret his genialis hiems,
laxat at arva tepens glacies,
floribu ut cumulet clathos.
  ista comantibus e foliis
munera, virgo puerque, date.

'Pluck ye purple violets, pick blood-red crocuses. Our genial winter
has no lack of them; the cold is tempered and loosens its grip on the
land to load our baskets with flowers. Give her these gifts, you girls
and boys, from the luxuriant leaves.'[26]

Some early medieval mysticism appeared toward the end of the
sixth century in Fortunatus' treatment of the Cross. And here, as in
the earlier work of Marius Victorinus during the fourth century, is
a possible anticipation of Old English poems centering around the
Cross. Mysticism is, of course, an extremely elusive term, and it
certainly seems valid to say that the medieval tendency toward
allegory and symbolism plus the asceticism of the monastic movement in the church, the growing cult of the martyrs, and the importance placed on such esoteric sources of knowledge as number
symbolism and astrology all contributed to a general literary atmosphere which might be described as mystic. Mysticism has what
might be called both formal and informal aspects. It began to
formalize early in the church in direct mystical experiences, of
which we have many records, not the least among which are some
of the writings of St. Augustine. This mysticism is the direct result
of a deliberate disassociation of oneself from the material or outer
world; it is obviously an outgrowth, at least in large part, of the monastic tradition. There is, however, that aspect of mysticism which,
although as directly rooted in spiritual experience as the more formal aspect, finds its expression in the world of men. This experience was the great motivating force which carried forward the
missionary movement of the church and manifested itself as the
truly self-sacrificing humility of the great monk-teachers, the
peregrini, in their at times miraculous achievements in conversion
of the heathen nations. The isolation of these men in the lonely
heathen lands lent a kind of elegiac flavor to their lives and to the

[26] Thomson, II, 154.

poetry which may well have been inspired by the lives they led, poems such as *The Wanderer* and *The Seafarer*.

There is ample evidence that all but three of the continental Christian Latin writers mentioned here were known in England early enough to have affected the development of the Old English poetic tradition. First, we have Alcuin's poetic listing of the authors in the York library, and, second, there is the evidence presented by J. D. A. Ogilvy in his study *Books Known to the English, 597–1066*.[27] Alcuin gives us the names of Lactantius, Marius Victor, Juvencus, Ambrose, Avitus of Vienne, Fortunatus, Paulinus of Nola, Sedulius, and Arator. Ogilvy shows evidence of knowledge in the Old English schools of every writer mentioned in this chapter except Cyprian, Paulinus of Perigueux, and Marius Victorinus. Alcuin states, however, that the works of Marius Victorinus were included in the York library. The most widely known writers seem to have been Ambrose, Juvencus, Prudentius, St. Hilary of Arles, Fortunatus, Paulinus of Nola, and Sedulius. Those of whom the Old English seem to have had a fair knowledge were Lactantius, Tino Prosper, Dracontius, and Arator. Those of whom they seem to have had less knowledge include Marius Victorinus, Ausonius, Marius Victor, and Avitus of Vienne. There are apparently no direct references in Old English writing to Cyprian or Paulinus of Perigueux. Of course, the people mentioned here must be taken in addition to the many others of whom there was a vast knowledge in the Old English libraries, men such as St. Jerome, St. Augustine of Hippo, St. Athanasius, Pope Gregory the Great, Pope Leo II, Bishop Basil of Caesarea, Orosius, St. John Chrysostom, Boethius, Cassiodorus, Virgil, Statius, Lucan, Donatus, Priscian, and others. Alcuin ends his poem concerning the library by saying that he has by no means listed all the works contained therein, that one will find there many other volumes by eminent schoolmasters. Even discounting possible prideful exaggeration, one wonders just who the others were. Be that as it may, there is sufficient evidence of the continuity of learning and literary tradition, from the time of the early Christian Latin writers on the continent to the time of the Old English poetic tradition, upon which to base an assumption

[27] (Cambridge, Mass., 1967).

of fairly wide influence of the older tradition upon the younger, in fact, of assuming that Old English poetry is part of the continuous tradition of Christian literature.

II

THE ELEGIES: AN INTRODUCTION

The poetry usually considered the earliest in the English language has long been a source of great debate, largely because of its appearance at a time when the people who wrote it were going through a transitional period of conversion from pagan belief to Christian. Both worlds are inevitably expressed in the poetry but the evaluation of their respective roles has been greatly complicated and confused.

It was the habit of earlier scholars such as Taine, ten Brink, Courthope, and Brooke to see all Old English poetry, including that of Caedmon and Cynewulf, as a heterogeneous mixture of heathen and Christian elements. More recent scholars, however, tend to place the work of Caedmon and Cynewulf and their 'schools' under the heading of Christian poetry and to discuss whether or not the epics and elegies, which probably came later, can be so designated. I shall not deal here with the argument concerning the epic. Of the elegies, I shall choose two with which to work in detail: *The Wanderer* and *The Seafarer*.

Since the mid-nineteenth century various approaches have been taken toward trying to understand these poems. Conclusions have been sharply contradictory largely because of the inability to recognize that the poems represent a culture, if not lost at least long forgotten, and that they, therefore, must be studied in as close to valid historical perspective as possible. Taine perhaps adumbrated this approach but then closed the door on himself by dismissing the work of art *per se* as useless, by insisting that its only reason for existence was as a clue to the man and the culture which had produced it.[1] Taine and most of the other scholars dismissed the Christianity present in the poems as later additions by Christian scribes and found that what they called the 'Christian coloring' had weakened if not destroyed the genius of the Saxon. Karl Müllenhoff popularized the theory of composite authorship and dissected the poems into a series of fragments and interpolations.[2] Müllenhoff greatly emphasized the oral tradition and insisted that the real poems lay somewhere behind the manuscript pieces with their interpolated Christian elements. However, since the oral versions of these works had probably disappeared long before the manuscripts as we have them were copied, the attempt to recreate the 'original poems' was rather like trying to grasp an image in water. The futility of the attempt is attested by the many conflicting conclusions drawn by those scholars as to the exact nature of the poetry.[3]

A few of the early scholars, however, argued that the poems could be read as complete and integral units. Thomas Arnold in 1876 argued that *Beowulf*, for instance, was a literary composition by a churchman.[4] John Earle in 1892 argued that the poem was composed at the Mercian court for the specific purpose of exemplifying the training of an ideal prince.[5] Both date the poem in the eighth century. Courthope, although he insisted on the poem's lack of plan and unity, agreed that the poet was a Christian and sang before a Christian audience, but denied that he was a churchman. Instead, he followed the insistence on the lateness of the oral tradition and saw the poet as a *scop*.[6]

Another of the early approaches was to interpret the poetry as myth. Müllenhoff originated the idea that the name Beowulf, for instance, was derived from *bhū* 'to grow', and came to the con-

---

[1] H. A. Taine, *History of English Literature*, trans. Henri van Laun (New York, 1873), p. 2.
[2] See, for instance, his study *Beovulf* (Berlin, 1888).
[3] For a brief summary of the attitudes toward the elegies, see Charles W. Kennedy, *The Earliest English Poetry* (New York, 1943), p. 101ff.
[4] Thomas Arnold, *Beowulf: A Heroic Poem of the Eighth Century, with a Translation, Notes, and Appendix* (London, 1876). Cited in John Earle, *The Deeds of Beowulf* (Oxford, 1892), pp. xliv-xlv.
[5] Earle, pp. lxxvff, especially p. xcv.
[6] W. J. Courthope, *History of English Poetry*, 6 vols. (New York, 1885), I, 90.

clusion that Beowulf represented settled culture, Grendel the North Sea with its inundations of the land, Grendel's mother the depths of the sea, and the dragon winter where God's (Beowulf's) power (fruitfulness) wanes.[7] This mythological interpretation was accepted by such scholars as ten Brink, Boer, Brooke, Ettmüller, and Symons. Those who follow this lead usually see the poem as part of ancient myth with Beowulf as the force of man (society) against the forces of nature which would destroy him and eventually do. The inevitability of destruction is seen as part of the fear and gloom which many scholars see as so essential a quality of early Germanic poetry.

Perhaps the earliest attempt to study the elegies as allegories was made in 1909 by Ehrismann.[8] In a now famous paper on *The Seafarer*, Ehrismann suggested that the sea voyage represents the afflictions of life. He also suggested that life on land is materialistic life as contrasted with life at sea, which represents a life of religious commitment. He suggested that the seafarer is a monk who finds the pleasures of the worldly life sinful. Furthermore, he stated that all 124 lines of the poem as it appears in *The Exeter Book* are unified and pervaded by a homiletic quality. Almost every aspect of Ehrismann's suggestions have been taken up since his time. The wide field of investigation he opened by linking the allegory with theology has proved perhaps the most fruitful of all attempts to arrive at a satisfactory interpretation of the Old English elegies.

Recent scholarship has, for the most part, tended to see the poems as unified works, although there remain a few voices supporting the idea that they are disjointed composites and that the Christianity present is there through later scribal interpolation, represented most forcefully by E. E. Wardale and George K. Anderson. The conclusion of recent scholars that the poems are unified wholes has given definite substantiation to the argument that they are Christian works composed by churchmen.

[7] See R. W. Chambers, *Beowulf, an Introduction*, 3rd ed. with a supplement by C. L. Wrenn (Cambridge, 1959), p. 46 and n.
[8] G. Ehrismann, "Religionsgeschichtliche Beiträge zum germanischen Frühchristentum", *Beiträge zur Geschichte der Deutschen Sprache und Literatur*, XXXV (1909), 209-239.

Contemporary scholarship has fallen into five fairly well defined attitudes. There are those who insist on a literal interpretation, represented by Dorothy Whitelock; those who see the poems as symbolic, represented by I. L. Gordon and S. B. Liljegren; those who consider the poems Christian consolation, represented by R. M. Lumiansky, James E. Cross, and Stanley B. Greenfield; those who see the poetry as Christian allegory, represented by O. S. Anderson, D. W. Robertson, Jr., Bernard Huppé, G. V. Smithers, Susie I. Tucker, and Cross; and those who are interested in studying the oralformulaic character of the language itself, represented by F. P. Magoun, Jr., Robert P. Creed, and others.

Whitelock, speaking for the 'literalists', holds that a poem such as *The Seafarer* is a poem about an Old English *peregrinus*. According to her interpretation, the exile might be a monk bent on missionary work as a way to insure his personal salvation, or he might be a layman going on a pilgrimage to a distant shrine with the same idea in mind. To substantiate her theory she points to the many known instances of wandering missionaries in the early church, particularly Irish and English, and to existing records of pilgrimages by laymen of the period. She explains the seafarer's hesitancy by saying that it is normal for a man to hesitate to leave a life of physical comfort, that his trepidation is his recognition of the life of hardship upon which he is voluntarily embarking.

I. L. Gordon speaks for those who feel that the poetry is symbolic. Of course, when one is dealing with a term such as 'symbolic' one cannot afford to be too exclusive in setting up categories of critical attitude. Given the nature of art, all critics will perhaps see a degree of what they would call symbolism or figurativeness in a poem. However, Gordon takes as a point of departure a fundamental disagreement with those who hold that the work is Christian allegory.[9] The allegory, she argues, is not explicit in the poems, and she further argues that the tone of lament suggests elegy rather than allegory. She rejects Whitelock's literal interpretation of *The*

---

[9] In an early paper, "Traditional Themes in *The Wanderer* and *The Seafarer*", *RES*, n.s., V (1954), 1-13, Gordon characterizes O. S. Anderson's allegorical interpretation as "tortuous" and argues against interpreting the poems as wholly Christian. In her edition of *The Seafarer* (1960), however, she is more agreeable to the allegorical interpretation.

Seafarer, finding that the seafarer's reflections do not suggest the same kind of spiritual attitude found in the Irish hermit poems. She finds that the emphasis upon the imagery of the sea keeps what would be the more explicit allegorical context in the background, that the allegory never comes to the surface.

Lumiansky and Cross have argued in favor of the theme of Christian consolation. Lumiansky has found his substantiation largely within the theme and structure of the works themselves while Cross has based his argument on the existence of the *consolatio* genre in medieval Latin writing. Cross finds the *consolatio* flourishing in both pagan and Christian writing of the early Middle Ages and suggests that the Old English poets were aware of it as a general idea that pervaded the medieval intellectual climate. Lumiansky argues that the poets probably knew and read Boethius and found there a source for the consolation theme. The consolation theme which Cross finds in a poem such as *The Wanderer* is a more formal and stoic consolation, centered in the notion that if a man in a desperate situation can find no consolation personally he can at least take consolation in the fact that misery is the common condition of man. According to Cross' interpretation, the wanderer may also take consolation from the decaying condition of the world about him, since this decay emphasizes even more the condition of the entire universe as it approaches its end.[10] Lumiansky does not develop the consolation as stoicism, but emphasizes the Boethian motif of a conflict between the false felicity of the glory of earth and the true felicity of the glory of heaven. The wanderer, Lumiansky argues, is a man who has had the misery and transience of earthly glory and happiness brought so forcefully home to him that he turns at last to the awareness that the only true happiness is in heaven with the blessed.[11]

---

[10] For a development of the eschatological theme, see G. V. Smithers, "The Meaning of *The Seafarer* and *The Wanderer*", *MAE*, XXVI (1957), 137-153, and XXVIII (1959), 1-22.

[11] R. M. Lumiansky, "The Dramatic Structure of the O. E. Wanderer", *Neophil.*, XXXIV (1956), 104-112. Also see T. C. Rumble, "From *Eardstapa* to *Snottor on mode*: The Structural Principle of 'The Wanderer' ", *MLQ*, XIX (1958), 225-230.

The historical-allegorical approach to the poems is the approach which has gained the most of recent scholarly attention, and is perhaps, at this time, the most controversial. It goes ultimately back to the suggestion of Ehrismann in 1909 that *The Seafarer* is an allegory. Robertson, Smithers, Huppé, Cross, and Tucker have followed this lead and have studied thoroughly the cultural backgrounds of the early Middle Ages in order to place the poems in their proper relation to that background. It is this approach which I find the most fruitful since it seems to resolve ambiguities in interpretation which other approaches have failed to resolve. Without the cultural frame of reference, critics have been too apt to wander off into personal likes and dislikes.

Before proceeding to the work on the individual poems, I would like to point out what I consider one of the major weaknesses in the scholarship on these poems, a weakness which I shall deal with at greater length in my analyses. This weakness was particularly prevalent among earlier scholars but is still noticeable in recent research. The weakness is the failure to see the connection between Christian elements in the poems and Christian themes. Most early scholars, and a few recent ones, find Christian 'elements' and seem satisfied to stop without questioning the reasons for their being there, without assuming that the elements they find must be part of a larger whole which is the theme of the poem. Although this tendency has disappeared to some extent with the rise in popularity of the allegorical approach, I think that it remains hidden beneath the surface of much recent scholarship where it operates silently as a given assumption. In the work of Wardale and George K. Anderson this assumption is still obvious and active, but even in the excellent work of Whitelock the notion seems to be quietly at work molding the conclusion that the Christian themes are perhaps not essential after all, in spite of the presence of the elements. Whitelock argues against the necessity of an exclusively Christian theme, either symbolic or allegorical, in her literal interpretation. A quarter of a century before, Frederick Klaeber, in his four papers "Die christlichen Elemente im 'Beowulf' ", had dealt with the literalist argument and concluded that the *Beowulf* poet was not only an ecclesiast but a teacher without equal in Old English,[12] but until fairly recently not many scholars have been willing to follow his lead. It seems an unavoidable conclusion that if Christian elements are present in the poems, and even the most ardent of those who hold for paganism agree that they are, they must be there for a purpose. Since a poem can be literally no more than the figures and images which make it up, these elements can be nothing less than at least an attempt to build a meaningful structure. We need not at this time attempt the critic's job of evaluating the success or failure of such structures, but we must as scholars, it seems to me, admit the fact of their existence.

To arrive at an exact date of composition of any of the elegies is impossible. It is sufficient to say that most authorities agree that they were composed during the first half of the eighth century. L. L. Schücking dates *The Wanderer* in the late tenth century, but he is out of line with most scholarly opinion.[13] My point here can be simply stated. It is that most scholars agree that the poems were composed sometime after the establishment of the great monastic schools and libraries and well after the beginning of the tradition of Christian poetry in England. Scholars such as G. K. Anderson insist on a distinction between a poem's being composed and its being written down from a supposed oral tradition. I consider this distinction a nebulous one for two reasons: no one has yet proved conclusively the existence of such an oral tradition in connection with these elegies, and if one could be proved, I would question its relevance, since it seems reasonable to assume that the writing was done in a monastic center and would, therefore, involve a completely new use of the old materials for completely different purposes.

The presence of a Christian theme in the elegies can be argued successfully on two grounds: from internal evidence and from careful consideration of the intellectual context in which they were written. I shall reserve the argument from internal evidence for

---

[12]   Frederick Klaeber, "Die christlichen Elemente im Beowulf", *Anglia*, XXXV (1911), 111-135, 249-270, 453-482, and XXXVI (1912), 169-199.
[13]   Aldo Ricci, "The Chronology of Anglo-Saxon Poetry", *RES*, V (1929), 258.

consideration in the following chapter. However, the two areas of internal analysis and cultural background do overlap significantly in a way that can be pointed out here. The church-dominated culture in which our poets lived provided them with the imagic patterns in terms of which they saw experience. Two of the most universal of such patterns were those of the exile and of the gradual decay of the material world. The latter of these patterns involves us in the pervasive theological concern with eschatology. Both of the patterns, exile and eschatology, bring home the theme of the transience of earthly glory. The thematic pattern of the exile has always been recognized as the main theme of *The Wanderer,* for instance, but not until recently in the theological sence. The images of decay, destruction, and death, however, have occasioned a great amount of as yet unreconciled conflicting opinion. Eschatological images abound in the poem, occurring at two climactic passages, lines 58–63 and 73–107, but it has been usual for scholars to pass over these lines, commenting only on their power.

The Christian elegy was well known on the continent during the centuries just preceding the development of the Old English literary tradition and the works of the elegists were available in the English libraries. The earliest known was that of Paulinus of Nola, 353–431 A.D. Paulinus was well known in England by both Aldhelm and Bede. He was a particular favorite of Bede. Another poet known in England who wrote elegiac verse was Dracontius. His *Satisfactio* addressed to the vandal king Gunthamund contains these lines toward its end:

omnia cum redeant, homini sua non redet eatas,
    sed velut acris avis sic fugitiva volat.

'though all things return, man's life does not
        come back to him,
    but like a bird of passage upon swift wing, it
            flies away.' [14]

The lines are reminiscent of the passage in Bede in which one of Edwin's thanes compares human life to the flight of a swallow. The presence of the work of these two continental writers alone is

[14] Dracontii, *Satisfactio*, ed. and trans. Sister M. St. Margaret, Univ. of Pa. Dissertation (Philadelphia, 1936), lines 255-256.

enough to substantiate the familiarity of the English with a classical elegiac tradition during the century in which it is generally agreed that the Old English elegies were written. However, the classical tradition is not the only source of the elegiac strain in Old English poetry. The note of elegiac sadness is to be found in the asceticism of the church. We need only look at the lives of some of the great Irish and British saints such as Columba, Aidan, Cuthbert, and Boniface, men who for the glory of God imposed upon themselves exile and unbelievable hardship. Add to these facts the background of Teutonic myth and the bleak and wintry landscape of Northumbria and the elegiac atmosphere of poems such as *The Wanderer, The Seafarer,* and *The Ruin* is much easier to understand.

In saying this I do not align myself with those who have said that Old English poetry is bleak and gloomy. There is too much in the work to disprove such statements. The elegiac mood may contain sadness as one of its major ingredients, but with strict philosophic fatalism it seems to have no truck, certainly not the Christian elegy.

The definitions of historical criticism are many and varied but a definition at once simple and inclusive may serve us at this point. It is supplied by D. W. Robertson, Jr., in prefacing his remarks concerning *The Wanderer.* Historical criticism is defined by Robertson as "literary analysis which seeks to reconstruct the intellectual attitudes and the cultural ideals of a period in order to reach a fuller understanding of its literature".[15] With this definition in mind, some preliminary statements concerning allegorical interpretation can be made.

The most important doctrine preached by the church during the Middle Ages was that of charity, the law of the New Testament which was given in order to add new life and meaning to the law of the Old Testament. St. Augustine based his approach to the methods of study and learning on this doctrine, an approach which shaped his discussion of words as 'figures' and 'signs', and his discussion of the levels of meaning to be found in literature. A word

[15] D. W. Robertson, Jr., "Historical Criticism", *English Institute Essays* (1950), p. 5.

as 'figure' could be discussed only as the word itself; here questions
of form, syntax, or etymology were relevant. A word as 'sign' was
taken to signify something other than itself and could, therefore,
be discussed on the figurative as well as the literal level of meaning.
As a 'sign', a word could have, beyond the literal, three levels of
meaning: the tropological (level of the individual), the allegorical
(level of society), and anagogical (level of the eternal). Any one
word might have all three levels of significance to the reader
of continental or Old English medieval literature. Robertson uses
the word *Jerusalem* to point out the different levels of signification.
Taken as a 'figure' (by etymology), the word means 'City of
Peace', taken as a 'sign', it could signify the Christian ideal of
peace on all three levels, the individual (the human being), the
social (the church universal), and the eternal (God's infinite
mercy). A medieval audience would have been aware of these
levels of meaning although they may not seem apparent to a twentieth-century reader. The possibility of reading words on these
various levels in one and the same context was the foundation of
the allegorical method of interpretation which dominated the entire
medieval scene.

Robertson points to two other terms which have relevance to
the discussion of poetry: 'cortex' (the surface or literal meaning of
a work), and 'nucleus' (the deeper or figurative meaning). St.
Augustine, in his *De Doctrina Christiana,* equates these terms
respectively with eloquence (possibly empty or meaningless) and
truth. All such levels of meaning and figurative terms are part of
the allegorical approach to interpetation.

There are numerous examples of the allegorical in early Christian writing on the continent, many of them earlier than the work
of St. Augustine. The homilies of Ambrose relied heavily on allegory, a method which Ambrose had borrowed from the Greek
fathers. Reference has already been made to the *Phoenix,* attributed
to Lactantius, the *Psychomachia* and *Cathemerinon* of Prudentius,
the *De Pascha,* attributed to Marius Victorinus, and to the fragment *De Iona,* of uncertain authorship. The final lines of the *De
Iona* fragment state directly their allegorical application to the
resurrection of Christ. Prudentius uses the allegorical approach in

his *Contra Symmachum,* in which he attacks the old state reli-
gions by picturing the church as Paul, safe in harbor after a ship-
wreck, being attacked suddenly by a viper.[16] The work of Venan-
tius Fortunatus also contains much use of the allegorical method,
particularly in an elegiac poem on the Easter festival addressed to
Bishop Felix, which opens with the following lines, perhaps
slightly reminiscent of the well known elegiac passage in *The Seafarer* which describes the waxing and blooming of the world in
spring:

> mollia purpureum pingunt violaria campum,
> > prata virent herbis et micat herba comis.
> paulatim subeunt stellantia lumina florum
> > arridentque oculis gramina tincta suis.[17]

> 'Soft violets paint the purple plain,
> > the meadows are green with grasses and the
> > > friendly grass shimmers.
> Little by little spring up the starry lights
> > of flowers
> and the grasses laugh, colored with their eyes.'[18]

Flowers are traditionally associated with the elegiac mood and the
suggestion of fast fading beauty. All these poems illustrate the
allegorical method which St. Augustine stated in the *De Doctrina
Christiana* and which was the essence of the teaching of Pope
Gregory the Great, who passed it along to England with St.
Augustine of Canterbury. In England it appears in the work of
such men as Aldhelm and Bede, men who helped set the intellectual background against which much Old English poetry was
written.

I mentioned above two specific patterns of images which are
given meaning in the historical context: the image of the *peregrinus*
and the image pattern of decay and destruction which heralds the
end of the world. The pattern of the *peregrinus* is one of the con-
sistent symbolic patterns in medieval Christianity. It is found not

---

[16] Prudentius, *Contra Symmachum,* ed. H. J. Thomson, 2 vols. (Cambridge, Mass., 1940), I, 344; II, 97.
[17] F. J. E. Raby, *A History of Christian-Latin Poetry,* 2nd ed. (Oxford,
1953), p. 92.
[18] I am indebted to Professor Joseph P. Poe, formerly of the University of
Texas, for help in the translation of several Latin verses.

only in literary works of the period but throughout the corpus of medieval sermons and other ecclesiastical writings. In literary work, the figure is found as early as Commodian, who lived in the third century, in his *Instructiones (Instructions Written in Favor of Christian Discipline)*, a long didactic poem in acrostics, in the preface of which he states:

> Prima praefatio mostra viam arrenti demonstrat
> Respectumque bonum, cum venerit saeculi meta,
> Aeternum fieri, quod discredunt inscia corda.
> Ego similiter erravi tempore multo.

> 'My preface sets forth the way to the wanderer,
> and a good visitation when the goal of life shall
>   have come,
> that he may become eternal – a thing which ignorant
>   hearts disbelieve.
> I in like manner have wandered for a long time.' [19]

The figure is ultimately dependent upon the Bible, where we find man constantly being described as a wanderer, an exile in the world. In Christian interpretation, Adam is, of course, the first of the biblical wanderers, after his expulsion from Eden. The figure spreads throughout Scripture and throughout the vernacular as well as the patristic tradition. The wanderings of such men as Abraham and Moses, to name only two, are connected with the *peregrinus* figure. In the New Testament, the going out of the apostles into new and foreign lands to teach the gospel of Jesus is the same *peregrinus* pattern, especially the travels of Peter and Paul. The similarity of such figures to the *peregrini* of the eighth- and ninth-century British church is obvious. In the patristic tradition the figure appears in England, for instance, in Aelfric's homily on Shrove Sunday,[20] and in Blickling Homily X,[21] these uses taking as their possible source the opening of Book IV of Gregory's *Dia-*

[19] Commodian, *The Instructions of Commodianus in Favor of Christian Discipline*, in: *The Ante-Nicene Fathers*, X vols., eds. Rev. Alexander Roberts and James Donaldson, rev. by A. Cleveland Coxe (Grand Rapids, 1968), IV, 203.
[20] Benjamin Thorpe (ed.), *The Homilies of the Anglo-Saxon Church*, 2 vols. (Aelfric Society, 1844-1846), I, 162.
[21] *The Blickling Homilies*, ed. R. Morris (London, 1967), p. 112. Rprt. in

logues.[22] In the Old English poetic tradition, the figure is to be found in *Genesis A,* 927 ff.:

> þu scealt oðerne   eðel secean
> wynleasran wic,   and on wræc hweorfan
> nacod niedwædla,   neorxwanges
> dugeðum bedæled;   ðe is gedal witod
> lices and sawle.[23]

> 'Thou shalt seek another, a friendless
> home; in nakedness and wretchedness shalt
> thou depart, deprived of the joys of
> paradise; assuredly shalt thy body
> and soul be sundered.'

We find the exile theme in many other Old English poems: *The Wanderer, The Seafarer, Widsith, Deor, The Husband's Message, The Wife's Lament, St. Guthlac, Andreas, Elene,* to name several.

From these citations we may assume that the figure was a common one during the earliest period of the Old English poetic tradition. Gregory, who used the figure many times, even hinted at it in the letter of encouragement which he sent to St. Augustine and his despairing monks when they expressed the desire to be recalled from their mission to the English. Gregory exhorted the monks to continue their journey that he might see the results of their labors "in our heavenly home".[24] He does not use the image of the *peregrinus* as such, but it is significant that the language of the letter indicates that it was a fundamental Christian assumption that man had a duty to carry out his earthly mission in order to achieve his place in the City of God.

---

1 vol. of *EETS,* O.S. Nos. 58 (1874), 63 (1876), 73 (1880).
[22]   St. Gregory the Great, *Dialogues,* trans. Odo John Zimmerman, O.S.B., in: *The Fathers of the Church,* 72 vols. (New York, 1947-   ), XXXIX, 189-190.
[23]   George Philip Krapp (ed.), *The Junius Manuscript,* Vol. 1 of *The Anglo-Saxon Poetic Records,* 6 vols. (New York, 1931-1953), p. 31. Translations from the Old English are mine unless otherwise indicated.
[24]   Bede, *A History of the English Church and People,* trans. Leo Sherley-Price (Baltimore, 1955), p. 67. J. A. Giles' revision of the J. Stevens translation in the Everyman edition, *Bede's Ecclesiastical History of the English Nation* (New York, 1970), p. 33, rprt. of the 1910 ed., reads "in the heavenly country".

The second pattern of images under consideration is that of the decay and degeneration of earthly things, a condition which meant to the early medieval man the imminence of the promised end of the world and the Second Coming of Christ. This pattern of images establishes the eschatological theme in the elegies, a theme which was of even more importance to the early medieval church than was the theme of the *peregrinus*, although it should be emphasized that the two were integrally connected, one usually implying the other, as, for instance, in Blickling Homily X. The eschatological theme, like that of the *peregrinus*, is ultimately scriptural, in this instance being based on the promise of Christ to return and upon the promised second destruction of the world. The theme of the imminent return of Christ was a common one already as early as the third century, as we can see, for instance, in Cyprian's Treatise VII, "On the Mortality", where he talks of the passing away of the world and says that "already heavenly things are taking the place of the earthly".[25] In his tract *Ad Demetrianum* he uses the analogy which was to become a commonplace in literature and find its way into Old English poetry and the poetry of the later Middle Ages, that between the condition of the earth in its final stage and the body of an aging man. Napier points out the same theme in England in the pseudo-Wulfstan Homily XXX and in the Wulfstan Homily XLIX.[26] Kluge finds it in a sermon in the MS Cotton Tiberius A III,[27] and Bede used it in *De Temporum Ratione*, where his concluding chapters deal with the Day of Judgment and the coming of Antichrist.[28] In these sources, and in many others which could be cited, several themes are common: the inevitable passage of time, the promised destruction of the world, the Second Coming, the millennial theory, the physical evidence of the approaching end of the world in the ruins which abound upon earth, the analogue between the old age of man and the old age of the earth, the terrors of the end of the world and

[25] In: *The Ante-Nicene Fathers*, eds. Roberts and Donaldson, V, 469.
[26] A. S. Napier, *Wulfstan* (Weimar, 1882), pp. 143ff and 150ff.
[27] Friedrich Kluge, "Zu altenglischen Dichtungen", *ES*, VIII (1885), 472-474.
[28] J. P. Migne, *Patrologia Cursus Completus*, series latina prima, 221 vols. (Paris, 1844-1864), XC, 520ff.

of the Day of Judgment to follow immediately, and the transience of all earthly goods. Not all of these ideas appear in each of the works, naturally, but they are all to be found as a part of the patristic and secular literary tradition of the time.

In the interpretations of the individual Old English elegies I shall try to show the existence of all these themes in such a way as to make reasonably certain that the elegies are part of the tradition of Christian writing which began on the continent during the third century.

III

THE WANDERER

Immediately noticeable in the opening five lines of *The Wanderer* is the theme of the man exiled from his former security and now wandering in search of a new and (it is to be assumed) more lasting source of the security and happiness which he has lost. The fact that there is evidence for believing that the poets who wrote these poems were monks makes it highly likely that the figure of the wanderer is to be connected with the allegory of the exile from paradise. It is equally likely that a Christian audience trained to think in terms of figurative, that is, allegorical meaning would have made the connection. The fact that this opening passage plus the closing lines of the poem are the only passages which the 'paganists' are willing to admit are Christian makes the argument for allegorical interpretation even stronger.

In the first five lines the wanderer begs for God's mercy during the time of his exile. The word *gebide* is sometimes translated 'awaits' or 'abides', and this meaning will fit the allegory equally well, since in any case the Christian *peregrinus* could be 'awaiting', 'biding', 'praying', or 'begging' God's mercy in his search for the way to salvation. R. W. V. Elliott has remarked that the translation of *are* as 'mercy' overlooks the pagan meaning of the word, 'honor', 'glory', or 'dignity'.[1] However, the ideas of 'honor' or 'glory' fit as well in the allegorical interpretation as 'mercy', and the idea of 'dignity' only slightly less so. It seems reasonable enough that the wanderer should pray for the honor or glory of God's grace, a gift which certainly adds to the dignity of a man. The word *are*, however, has what seems to me a more fascinating

[1] R. W. V. Elliott, "The Wanderer's Conscience", *ES*, XXXIX (1958), 198.

function in the passage. It is an example of the subtle humor of the Old English poet, a humor too often overlooked by critics. The word is a perfect pun: it can be translated 'oar' in addition to the other suggested readings. An oar to a man exiled on the sea might well fit into the allegory as symbolic of the rod or the staff of the Lord which would give him support on his way, and in this particular wanderer's situation it would be even more welcome, since it is specifically stated that he moves over the ice-cold sea by means of his hands. The pun may explain what has appeared to most translators as a troublesome vagueness in line four.

It is necessary that a connection be established between sea imagery and the figure of the exile. Sea imagery abounds in patristic and homiletic writing of the early Middle Ages. It appears in such abundance, in fact, that it is perhaps tantamount to insisting on a truism to refer to specific examples. Many images of the sea and man as the searcher for his heavenly home occur, of course, in the Bible. For instance, patristic writings allegorically interpret passages such as Matthew 14:27-33, Mark 4:36-39, and 6:45-52, Luke 8:22-25, and John 6:16-21. Images of the searcher, which provide the *peregrinus* theme, are to be found at John 14:1-4 and Hebrews 11:10, 13-16, and 13:14. The figures of the exiled searcher and the sea become associated early in the patristic tradition, where the sea is interpreted as human life with its unpredictableness and hardship, upon which the exile must make his way. Cyprian makes reference to the storms of the world[2] and Origen uses the symbolism of the sea of life in his commentary on Matthew.[3] Very soon in patristic writing the ship became associated with the church,[4] an association which rounded out the theological allegory by linking the aspirations of the individual with the institution. The existence of these ideas in the cul-

[2] In: Roberts and Donaldson, *The Ante-Nicene Fathers*, V, "On the Unity of the Church", p. 421, "On the Dress of Virgins", p. 430, "On the Mortality", p. 469.
[3] Origen, *Commentary on Matthew* [13:47], trans. Rev. John Patrick, in: *The Ante-Nicene Fathers*, X vols., V.10, Original Supplement to the American Edition, ed. Allan Menzies (Grand Rapids, 1969), 420.
[4] Smithers, "The Meaning of *The Seafarer* and *The Wanderer*", *MAE*, XXVIII (1959), 1-5.

ture and the literary tradition which produced the poems makes reasonable the association of the *anhaga* of the Old English elegy with the Christian allegorial figure of the exile from paradise.

The use of the word *wyrd* in line five still occasions in some quarters doubt as to the Christian theme; however, numerous scholars have pointed out the rapid assimilation by Christianity of terms which had originally been part of the pagan Germanic mythological vocabulary.[5] *Wyrd* here is easily translatable as 'Providence'. Even if the word 'fate' is insisted upon, the Christian idea is still seen in its suggestion of the controlling hand of God in all human experience. To such a man as the wanderer, the Christian *peregrinus*, his fate is certain – Holy Scripture has left no doubt as to the true condition of human life in this world.

Robertson makes an interesting observation on lines six and seven:

> Swa cwæð eardstapa,   earfeþa gemyndig,
> wraþra wælsleahta,   winemæga hryre [6]

> 'So spoke a wanderer,   mindful of sufferings,
> of grievous slaughters   the fall of kinsmen.'

by recalling the distinction between the cortex and the nucleus of a piece of writing. The cortex of these lines is a reference to the Germanic comitatus life, and Robertson holds that, on the surface, this is what the poet had in mind. However, he continues, the nucleus of the lines is the exile's realization that in the battle against cupidity in self and against Satan in the universe many men fall, a thought which disturbs him greatly.[7] To see these lines as representing the battle against cupidity and Satan is to make use of the words as signs. Each of the key words in the passage carries the double meaning. The *eardstapa* is both the Germanic exile and the Christian *peregrinus*; *earfeþa* indicates both the miseries of the comitatus exile and the hardships of the man exiled from paradise; *waelsleahta* indicates both the slaughters of the battlefield and the deaths

---

[5] See, for instance, B. J. Timmer, "Wyrd in Anglo-Saxon Prose and Poetry", *Neophil.*, XXVI (1941), i, 24-27; ii, 27-33; iii, 213-228.
[6] All quotations from *The Wanderer* are from George Philip Krapp and Elliott Van Kirk Dobbie (eds.), *The Exeter Book*, Vol. III of *The Anglo-Saxon Poetic Records*, 6 vols. (New York, 1931-1953).
[7] Robertson, "Historical Criticism", p. 19.

of those who die in pilgrimage in the battle against evil – monks, missionaries, lay pilgrims –, and *winemaega* indicates both blood kinsmen of the tribe and brother pilgrims who have fallen in the search for salvation. Even the idea of the fallen suggests the double meaning of those who have met physical martyrdom and those for whom the rigors of the pilgrimage have proven too much and who have turned back.

The poem up to this point has been a general statement about a human being in a desperate situation, a human being who has had the very foundation of his faith and security torn away. The lines that follow begin a personal statement of the same situation. The intimacy of the statement makes the tone of despair even more intense.

> "Oft ic sceolde ana   uhtna gehwylce
> mine ceare cwiþan.   Nis nu cwicra nan
> þe ic him modsefan   minne durre
> sweotule asecgan.   (8-11a)

> 'Each morning I must in the loneliness before dawn,
> bemoan my sorrow. Nor is there now any alive
> to whom I can openly tell
> my inmost thoughts.'

As yet we have not been told the specific reason for this despair. We have, however, been made aware of the hard lot of the exile, of the misery of the human being who must accept the evil as well as the good which is dealt out by the hand of Providence. *Wyrd biδ ful araed!* There is, however, in the lines a significant image, one which, in spite of the depth of despair conveyed, prepares for the hope which will spring from the wanderer's experiences. I refer to the image of early morning in line 8b. On the literal level (the cortex) the wanderer is describing the darkness just before dawn, but on the deeper level (the nucleus) the darkness is the darkness of despair in the heart of the exile. But the image of dawn is what gives the lines their real meaning. Before dawn it is still dark, but we know that day will break, that light will come, indeed, that morning is imminent. Dawn as an allegorical sign is one of the oldest symbols of God's imminent presence in human experience. When the light comes, man's fear and despair retreat with the

darkness, and faith and security return. In his introductory remarks
to Book IV of the *Dialogues*, Gregory the Great uses the images
of darkness and light to symbolize sin and salvation. He refers to
Adam's being driven from the joys of paradise into "the distress
of this dark exile we are now suffering", and a few lines later he
uses the image of light in characterizing the presence of the Holy
Spirit.[8] So, even though we have the wanderer in the darkness of
despair, we are prepared for the coming of the Holy Spirit which
will return him to his faith.

The lines that follow present to us one of the points at which
those who hold for the heathen nature of the elegies find their
strongest substantiation.

> Ic to soþe wat
> þæt biþ in eorle   indryhten þeaw,
> þæt he his ferðlocan   fæste binde,
> healde his hordcofan,   hycge swa he wille.
> Ne mæg werig mod   wyrde wiðstondan,
> ne se hreo hyge   helpe gefremman.   (11b-16)

The word *indryhten* in this passage is regularly translated 'noble',
and interpreted as signifying the stoic virtue of self-discipline which
we are so used to associating with the comitatus culture. However,
the second element of the word, *dryhten*, is one of the most common Old English terms for God or Christ. The preposition *in*, here
used as a prefix, had the same significance in Old English as it has
in Modern English, 'in, into, at'.[9] The wanderer can just as easily
be saying that he knows it to be a God-like custom or virtue among
men of noble bearing not to give voice to their despair, not to resort
to self-pity. Despair is the state in which the soul of the Christian
is in the greatest danger of the sin of presumption, the one truly
unforgivable sin, for in that state, presuming to doubt even God's
mercy, it can neither face the hard facts of its earthly exile nor
help itself through prayer. Following is my translation of the lines,

---

[8] St. Gregory the Great, *Dialogues*, trans. Zimmerman, *The Fathers of
the Church*, XXXIX, 189-190.
[9] Joseph Bosworth, *An Anglo-Saxon Dictionary*, ed. and enlarged by
T. Northcote Toller (London, 1954), rprt. of 1898 ed. All references to word
meanings in Old English will be based upon this dictionary, which hereafter
will be referred to as Bosworth-Toller.

in which it seems to me, the Christian implications fit comfortably:

> 'I truly know
> that it is, in a noble man, a Godly custom
> that he his deepest thoughts bind fast,
> hold fast his heart, think what he will;
> neither can the despairing of heart withstand fate
> nor the troubled spirit bring help.'

The two lines following this passage are closely connected with it. They are usually translated in a negative sense, since it has become such an unquestioned custom to read Old English poetry, particularly the elegies, as dark, gloomy poems.

> Forðon domgeorne   dreorigne oft
> in hyra breostcofan   bindað fæste   (17-18)

These lines have always been troublesome to translators. In almost every instance there has seemed to be some elusive meaning in the passage with which the translator cannot come to grips. As a result, the lines have been rendered vaguely or ambiguously as an expression of gloom. Taken as such, they are assumed to mean that since there is no help but to remain stoically quiet about one's misery, those who wish to appear to have this noble virtue keep their troubles to themselves. Another interpretation is possible, however, if we accept the lines as part of the more positive context established by my translation of lines 11b-16. Following the wanderer's awareness that despair affords him no real help, these lines may be read to mean that the man who yearns for God's blessing and realizes that despair avails him nothing will refrain from self-pity. The lines are actually the concluding part of the thought expressed in lines 11b-16 and should be read with them.

> 'I truly know
> that it is, in a noble man, a Godly custom
> that he his deepest thoughts bind fast,
> hold fast his heart, think what he will;
> neither can the despairing of heart withstand fate
> nor the troubled spirit bring help.
> Therefore, the seekers after glory oft
> deep within their breasts bind fast their sadness.'   (11b-18)

This interpretation turns, like the one above, on recognizing a wider possible translation of a word than is usual, *domgeorne*. The first element of the word, *dom*, is usually interpreted to mean the authority of or honor due to a Germanic chief or thane, but as a whole word *dom* also signifies the judgment of God. Therefore, the lines can be read as the wanderer's conclusion that since despair cannot help him in his quest of God's mercy (the *are* of line one), the first step for a man who seeks God's blessing is to learn to control his feelings of anxiety concerning his own faith. As Robertson's suggestion concerning lines six and seven indicates, both levels of interpretation are possible, but it is reasonable to assume that an audience to whom the allegorical method of reading and teaching was tantamount to a way of life would have heard the theological overtones of such a situation.

Lines 19-29a are the wanderer's extended application to himself of the situation he has just described:

swa ic modsefan   minne sceolde,
oft earmcearig,   eðle bidæled,
freomægum feor   feterum sælan,
siþþan geara iu   goldwine minne
hrusan heolstre biwrah,   ond ic hean þonan
wod wintercearig   ofer waþema gebind,
sohte sele dreorig   sinces bryttan,
hwær ic feor oþþe neah   findan meahte
þone þe in meoduhealle   min mine wisse,
oþþe mec freondleasne   frefran wolde,
weman mid wynnum.

The words *eðle bidæled* at line 20b seem to me to be the key to the entire passage. The word *eðle* 'home' is customarily interpreted as signifying the earthly home, but there is extensive use of it in Old English as significant of the heavenly home or the home of the angels. The interpretation of *bidæled* is also significant in the allegorical context. The deprivation usually associated with the word is that of the loss of the comitatus lord (as suggested in lines 22-23a), but the deprivation fits equally well the situation of the descendant of Adam deprived of paradise. The *goldwine minne* referred to at line 22b is on the cortex level the comitatus lord, but on the nucleus level would probably have been understood by the contemporary audience to refer to God or Jesus, as well. In this instance, the death of the gold friend can be read allegorically as the crucifixion of Jesus. It is the very fact of the crucifixion and the absence of immediate succor which the wanderer feels so acutely. It is a common and realistic human situation. Robertson makes a significant point concerning these lines.[10] He refers to a commonplace of medieval exegesis and teaching which centers in the interpretation of St. Paul's Epistle to the Romans 6:3-6:

3 Know you not that all we who are baptized in Christ Jesus are baptized in his death?

4 For we are buried together with him by baptism into death: that, as Christ is risen from the dead by the glory of the Father, so we also may walk in newness of life.

5 For if we have been planted together in the likeness of his death, we shall be also in the likeness of his resurrection.

6 Knowing this, that our old man is crucified with him, that the body of sin may be destroyed, to the end that we may serve sin no longer.[11]

The epistle indicates another possible level of complexity in the poem. St. Paul makes a direct association of the crucifixion with baptism. The Old English audience would have taken the reference to the death of the lord (Lord-Christ) as a reference to the sacrament of baptism, specifically, to the baptism of the wanderer. According to Christian teaching, the wanderer would have begun his exile at the time of his baptism. By accepting the sacrament of baptism man accepts his lot as the descendant of Adam. To a man of the Middle Ages this acceptance would have meant, much more than it does to modern man, a deprivation of primal security, a turning out (though with the strength of God's presence in His sacrament) into the darkness of the threat of doubt and despair, to seek for himself his way back to his heavenly home. Lines 23b-29a reemphasize the state of exile.

Three points in the passage deserve further comment: the words *gebind* and *bryttan* and the phrase *weman mid wynnum*. Both Gollancz and R. K. Gordon translate *gebind* 'frozen', and Kennedy

[10] Robertson, "Historical Criticism", p. 20.

[11] The Douay-Rheims translation is being used because of its faithfulness in rendering the Vulgate, the Bible used during the Middle Ages.

avoids the word entirely.[12] It seems to me that the word implies literally the surface of the waves. This very literalness, however, makes possible a double level of interpretation. As has been pointed out, the sea in patristic writing has been associated with life, an association which fits the allegorical situation of the wanderer. In allegorical writing, the surface is the allegory. As regards *bryttan*, scholars have consistently overlooked significant aspects of the word's meaning. Here, I think, is an example of the tendency of scholarship not to question established or traditional interpretations. *Bryttan* is regularly translated 'giver of treasure' or 'treasure-giver', signifying the comitatus prince, as by Gollancz and R. K. Gordon. However, Bosworth-Toller gives numerous examples from Old English poetry in which the word is used to signify either the devil or God: *synna brytta* 'the prince of sin'; *morðres brytta* 'the prince of murder'; *lifes brytta* 'the giver of life'; *swægles brytta* 'the Lord of Heaven'. In the first two phrases the word could just as easily be translated 'giver', in the third 'prince', and in the fourth either 'giver' or 'prince'. The frequent associations of the word with spiritual being would seem to indicate that its spiritual significance is equally as important as its physical. If this be so, the word substantiates the allegorical interpretation of the passage. The *sinces brytta* whom the wanderer seeks is not only an earthly lord but also the Lord of the City of God, and *sinces* refers to the wanderer's personal salvation. I think we may dismiss the possibility of his seeking Satan. Finally, in the phrase *weman mid wynnum*, the word *weman* has been a thorn to translators. They have regularly been unwilling to accept the most common meanings, 'to allure, attract, persuade, entice', and have translated 'cheer' or 'treat'. The unwillingness to accept the most common meanings seems to stem from the preconceived notion that the wanderer is the comitatus exile searching for a lord who at this point in the poem does not exist and who, if he did exist, would not evince the desire indicated in *weman* which would lead him in

[12] Isreal Gollancz (ed.), *The Exeter Book*, Pt. I (= *EETS*, O.S. 104) (London, 1905), p. 287; R. K. Gordon (trans.), *Anglo-Saxon Poetry* (London, 1926), p. 81; Charles W. Kennedy (trans.), *An Anthology of Old English Poetry* (New York, 1960), p. 5.

any way to urge the exile to join him. However, if we accept the possibility of allegorical interpretation (which both *gebind* and *bryttan* substantiate), the lord being sought may well be the Lord who exists for all time, and who moreover, would certainly so desire the presence of the exile that He would 'allure, attract, persuade', or 'entice' him to follow the path to salvation. The situation of the wanderer at this point is precisely that of the Christian after baptism, in which sacrament he has obliged himself to seek salvation and who, in turn, is sought by God as a sheep lost from the fold. Following is my translation of lines 19-29a:

> 'so I my inmost thoughts must,
> oft sad at heart, deprived of home,
> far from kinsmen, bind with fetters,
> since long ago my kindly lord
> was covered by the darkness of the earth, and I departed abject,
> possessed of wintry sadness, over the surface of the waves;
> drearily I sought the hall of a giver of treasure,
> where I, far or near, might find
> one who in the meadhall might know me
> or comfort me, the friendless one,
> lure me with delights.'

Lines 29b-36 state the cavalier manner with which the wanderer in his youth accepted the goods of the earth.

> Wat se þe cunnað,
> hu sliþen bið   sorg to geferan,
> þam þe him lyt hafað   leofra geholena.
> Warað hine wræclast,   nales wunden gold,
> ferðloca freorig,   nalæs foldan blæd.
> Gemon he selesecgas   ond sincþege,
> hu hine on geoguðe   his goldwine
> wenede to wiste.   Wyn eal gedreas!

A man in his youth has not yet learned the lesson of earth's transience. However, the outcry of line 36b tells us that years have brought the knowledge that earth's treasures are fragile and fleeting when compared with the everlasting love of God. Anyone, the wanderer says, who has realized this truth and has put it to the test knows the sorrow and hardship that make up the necessary state of the penitent. *Wyn eal gedreas!*

The translation of *goldwine* in this passage presents a problem.

Whereas previous references to the prince or lord have been shown to suggest Godhead, this reference more strongly suggests the earthly prince. I see in the word a possible deliberate ambiguity. The poet could here be referring to both the earthly and heavenly lords at once. If so, the double meaning would produce a definitely ironic effect. Not only has the wanderer as a youth been cavalier in accepting the earthly rewards bestowed upon him by his earthly leader, he has also been cavalier in accepting thoughtlessly the spiritual rewards signalled by the sacrament of baptism. He not only would, on the literal level, have been dealt a grievous blow by the death of the earthly prince and the concomitant realization that earthly life and goods are insubstantial and that death is inevitable; but also, on the allegorical level, by the association of the death of the earthly prince with the more meaningful death of the heavenly prince, which would bring home to him the urgency of his need to seek a more enduring reward before it is too late. One other word in the passage seems to have an ironic double meaning, *waraδ* of line 32a. The word demands in its context a translation of 'remains', but the form *warian* also means 'to beware, to make aware, to warn'. The double meaning in the passage is justified if we realize that the death of the prince (allegorically, the wanderer's baptism) and his resulting exile, the isolation associated with which suggests his growing self-consciousness as to his spiritual state, must certainly add to a sense of urgency and anxiety which fits the situation of the exile:[13]

> 'He knows who understands
> how treacherous sorrow may be as a companion
> to one who has few beloved protectors.
> To him remains the exile's path, not the twisted gold;
> the chill of the body, not the rewards of earth.
> He remembers the retainers, the receiving of treasure,
> how in his youth his goldfriend
> rewarded him at the feasting. All joy has passed away!'

The following lines, 45-57, contain two problems, one of them an important crux of the poem.

[13] Stanley B. Greenfield has noted this same kind of word-play in the latter part of *The Seafarer*, see "Attitudes and Values in 'The Seafarer'", *SP*, LI (1954), 18ff.

Ðonne onwæcneð eft   wineleas guma,
gesihð him biforan   fealwe wegas,
baþian brimfuglas,   brædan feþra,
hreosan hrim ond snaw,   hagle gemenged.
Þonne beoð þy hefigran   heortan benne
sare æfter swæsne.   Sorg bið geniwad,
þonne maga gemynd   mod geondhweorfeð;
greteð gliwstafum,   georne geondsceawað
secga geseldan.   Swimmað eft on weg!
Fleotendra ferð   no þær fela bringeð
cuðra cwidegiedda.   Cearo bið geniwad
þam þe sendan sceal   swiþe geneahhe
ofer waþema gebind   werigne sefan.

The first problem centers in the word *onwæcneð*, line 45. The word is regularly translated 'awakens', as though the wanderer were waking from a sleep. There is nothing, however, in the previous lines to indicate that he has just been asleep. The only ones which might be taken to indicate his sleeping at this point are lines 37–40, particularly line 39a:

Forþon wat se þe sceal   his winedryhtnes
leofes larcwidum   longe forþolian,
ðonne sorg ond slæp   somod ætgædre
earmne anhogan   oft gebindað.   (Italics mine)

However, the 'when' clause here seems to be part of the wanderer's general comment on the condition of all men like himself rather than a reference to himself at this specific moment. A lonely man, he is saying, will often think of his past and his lost comrades and be troubled by sorrowful dreams. He has been indulging in reverie, but there is nothing at this point, I think, to indicate that he is sleeping. *Onwæcnan* also means 'arise'. Since a sitting position is one frequently assumed during periods of reverie, it seems reasonable to suggest that the lines mean simply that the wanderer rises from where he has been sitting and looks again at the lonely sea. I have accordingly translated *onwæcneð* 'rises'.

The major crux of the passage, and one of the major cruces of the poem, is the interpretation of lines 50-55, which contain the baffling image of the swimming and floating companions. Recent scholarship has tried to solve the problem in three ways: first, by assuming that the wanderer sees actual men aboard other ships; second, that the wanderer is talking of images of past companions (perhaps long dead) which he sees in a half-waking state or in his mind's eye; third, that the wanderer has cast a magic spell which calls back the bird spirits of his companions.[14] The third suggestion requires elaboration. Vivian Salmon, who made the suggestion, points to the belief in Old Norse and Old Icelandic that the soul could, on occasion, go outside the body in different shapes, human, animal, or bird. She has found evidence that the same belief existed in England. She cites the commonplace situation in Old Icelandic in which a person practicing a magic spell can call such spirit shapes from far away. Miss Salmon centers her argument on a suggested translation of the word *gliwstafum*. Most translators give a reading suggesting joy, glee, or rapture, but since this is the word's only appearance in Old English poetry the translation must remain conjectural. Salmon points out a possible connection of the word with *galere* 'magician', or *gealdor* 'spell', adding that these words are also connected with *galan* 'to sing'. She then suggests that the second element, *stafum*, means 'rune', since *stæf* shows many associations with magic practices. Since music and runes both have spiritual or magical connotations, Salmon interprets the lines as meaning that the wanderer has used a magic spell made with music runes in order to call to him the bird spirits of his companions. She suggests that where this may be a startling notion to the twentieth-century reader, it would have been a commonplace to the Old Icelandic or Old Norse reader, and possibly to the Old English. Her suggestion would solve the problem of the companions who both swim and float. It seems to me, however, somewhat over-erudite. If we return to the suggestion that the wanderer has not

---

[14] W. J. Sedgefield (ed.), *An Anglo-Saxon Book of Verse and Prose* (Manchester, 1928), p. 155, says the wanderer sees occupants of other vessels; W. J. B. Owen, "Wanderer, Lines 50-57", *MLN*, LXV (1950), 161-165, says the wanderer sees sailors as they come ashore; D. S. Brewer, "Wanderer, Lines 50-57", *MLN*, XLVII (1952), 398-399, compares the wanderer's situation with that of an old sailor in the poem "John Marr" by Herman Melville, in which the old sailor sees the forms of past companions swimming around him; Vivian Salmon, " 'The Wanderer' and 'The Seafarer' and the Old English Conception of the Soul", *MLR*, LV (1960), 1-10, suggests the magic spell.

been asleep at all, we are left with the probability of reverie images or hallucination. In this interpretation, the images conjured up by the words *swimmað* and *fleotendra* would be read figuratively as well as literally rather than exclusively literally, as they are by Salmon; the ideas of swimming and floating characterize vividly that vagueness peculiar to images which occur in reverie or hallucination. This reading of the words seems the simplest explanation. It also has the advantage of fitting the theme of loneliness which is so much a part of the Christian exile tradition:

> 'Then he rises again, the friendless man,
> sees before him dark waves,
> seabirds bathing, spreading their feathers,
> falling ice and snow mingled with hail.
> Then it is heavier, the heart pain,
> grievous for the loved one. Sorrow is renewed
> when the memory of kinsmen crosses his mind;
> he greets them with joy, looks upon them eagerly,
> speaks to the hall-companions. They swim away again;
> the spirit images do not there bring any
> familiar utterances; care is renewed
> in him who must send very frequently
> over the surface of the waves weary thoughts.'

The following lines, 58-65a, present two specific problems in translation, *færlice,* at line 61a, and *forþon* at lines 58a and 64a.

> Forþon ic geþencan ne mæg   geond þas woruld
> for hwan modsefa   min ne gesweorce,
> þonne ic eorla lif   eal geondþence,
> hu hi færlice   flet ofgeafon,
> modge maguþegnas.   Swa þes middangeard
> ealra dogra gehwam   dreoseð ond fealleþ,
> forþon ne mæg weorþan wis   wer, ær he age
> wintra dæl in woruldrice.

The translation of *forþon* in this passage has proved a major crux in the poem's interpretation. The wanderer at this point, after thinking about his personal situation, drawing certain generalizations about himself, and then considering his situation as part of the situation of the entire world, states for the first time some definite conclusion about his attitude. Depending to a large extent upon the translation of *forþon*, particularly at line 58a, the con-

clusion can be either positive or negative. If it is a negative conclusion, then the entire poem must remain a gloomy one, even in
spite of the Christian consolation passage which closes it. The
paganists as a rule hold with the gloomy reading and say that the
consolation in lines 111-15 is unmotivated and probably interpolated. However, if a positive reading is possible, and I think it
is, the passage becomes the turning point of the poem, anticipates
the further growth of the wanderer's awareness of his situation as
peregrinus which takes place in the lines which follow this passage,
and argues strongly for artistic unity of the whole.

Forþon has been translated variously as 'thus', 'and thus',
'verily', 'so', as well as the usual 'therefore'. Its most regular use is
as a causal conjunction, but the difficulty which a number of
scholars have encountered in finding smooth thematic development
in the passage has led to frequent attempts to force the word into
some other meaning. The differing translations lead, in turn, to
further contradictory interpretations. R. K. Gordon gives a translation similar to the one I shall suggest, finding the wanderer
abandoning his fatalistic attitude:

'And thus I cannot think why in this world my mind becomes not
overcast, when I consider all the life of earls, how of a sudden they
have given up the hall, courageous retainers. So this world each day
passes and falls; for a man cannot become wise till he has had his
share of years in the world.'[15]

Gordon interprets the wanderer as saying that he is not any longer
overcome when he considers the human lot, in other words, that
the wanderer is regaining his faith.

Kennedy, on the other hand, even though he translates *forþon*
'therefore', gives a negative interpretation:

'No wonder therefore,   in all the world,
If a shadow darkens   upon my spirit
When I reflect   on the fates of men –
How one by one   proud warriors vanish
From the halls that knew them,   and day by day
All this earth ages   and droops unto death.'[16]

---

[15]   R. K. Gordon (trans.), *Anglo-Saxon Poetry*, p. 82.
[16]   Kennedy (trans.), *An Anthology of Old English Poetry*, p. 6.

In this interpretation, the wanderer is still overcome with despair. Everything he has looked on and everything that has happened to him has convinced him that there is no hope.

Gollancz translated *forþon* 'verily' and settled for an ambiguous reading that can be either positive or negative:

> 'Verily I cannot imagine, as I survey this world,
> why my mind should not be saddened,
> when I fully consider the life of earls,
> how they have suddenly resigned their halls,
> brave-hearted fellows!' [17]

The modal construction "should not" avoids making the definite commitment to either sense of the passage. The conflicting translations and interpretations illustrated by the above three examples point up the crux.

In most passages where *forþon* appears, if the lines are studied carefully, the usual translation of 'therefore' will be found to fit, and such, I think, is the case here. The word here indicates that the thoughts which follow it result from the thoughts which immediately precede it, and the passage it introduces makes two important points: first, that the wanderer is not saddened by his experiences, and, second, that he for the first time realizes fully the significance of wisdom gained from experience. This theme of growing awareness leads directly to the final lines of the poem in which the *eardstapa* becomes *snottor on mode*, in which the man who had placed his faith in the false felicity of earthly things finds his true felicity in the things of the spirit.

Færlice means 'suddenly' or 'by chance' or 'unexpectedly'. The usual reading of 'suddenly' implies the other meanings in context. However, there is possibly more to the meaning of the word than that. *Fær* also means 'fear' or 'terror' or 'danger'. The connotations thus suggested add to the passage a tone of admonition, a tone most fitting to the situation in which the wanderer finds he must draw some conclusion as to himself and his future.

Finally, the lines have also another function: they introduce the eschatological motif, a motif directly related in medieval thinking and writing to the situation of the Christian exile. One of the most

[17] Gollancz (ed.), *The Exeter Book*, Pt. I, p. 289.

vivid impressions upon the mind of the wanderer is that of the physical condition of the world around him. He sees in it a general state of decay and degeneration, a state significant in the exegetical tradition of the sixth or last age of the world.[18] The impending end, the fear and suddeness of death, the transience of the earth, all urge the wanderer to haste in his search. The following translation emphasizes what I see as the turning point in the poem – the wanderer's realization that in spite of the bleakness of his condition and of his surroundings there is hope.

> 'Therefore, it amazes me that my thoughts
> about this world are not melancholy
> when I think about all the life of earls,
> how they so suddenly have fled the halls,
> the proud retainers. So this world
> each and every day rushes and falls.
> Verily, no man may grow wise e'er he age
> a deal of winters in this world.'

I have translated *forþon* at line 64a 'verily', where 'therefore' would have done just as well, in order to avoid what seemed a perhaps awkward repetition.

The rest of the poem is so closely knit thematically that it is all but impossible to discuss it piecemeal. The lines of generalization upon the necessity for wisdom blend into the eschatological theme, which moves without interruption into the closely related *ubi sunt* passage and on to the final consolation.

The passage of generalization, beginning at line 65b, because of its hortatory and aphoristic nature, has been interpreted by many as essentially pre-Christian. Passages of this type usually excite much searching for sources. Nora Kershaw found it to be a series of maxims in gnomic form, part of the heathen element and suggestive of the virtues associated with Teutonic aristocracy of pre-Christian times. This conclusion led her to compare the poem with *Beowulf* as a curious mixture of heathen themes and a few Christian additions.[19] Tucker, on the other hand, finds the ideas in the lines to be based on the wanderer's observation and experience. She finds

---

[18] Cf. Smithers' paper, fn. 4, above.
[19] Nora Kershaw, *Anglo-Saxon and Norse Poems* (Cambridge, 1922), pp. 1-3.

counterparts to the lines in *Proverbs* and *Ecclesiastes*, books which she terms pre-Christian "and indeed sub-Christian, but . . . part of the Canon".[20] At another point, she seems somewhat more convinced of their Christian application when she says that certainly Bishop Leofric of Exeter would not have accepted a book for his library which he felt contained ideas either inadequate or heretical. Elizabeth Suddaby points out a parallel in Wulfstan's *Sermo de Baptismate:*

> Ne beon ge ofermode ne to weamode ne to niðfulle
> ne to flitgeorne ne to felawyrde ne ealles to hlagole
> ne eft to asolcene ne to unrote. Ne beon ge to rance
> ne to gylpgeorne ne færinga to fægene ne eft to ormode.

'Be not too arrogant or ill-tempered or too envious or too quarrelsome, or too talkative or altogether too much inclined to laugh and then afterwards too sluggish and dejected. Be not too proud or too ready to boast, or too cheerful suddenly and then afterwards too despondent.'[21]

The Wulfstan passage may be compared with lines 65b-69 of *The Wanderer:*

> Wita sceal geþyldig,
> ne sceal no to hatheort   ne to hrædwyrde,
> ne to wac wiga   ne to wanhydig,
> ne to forht ne to fægen,   ne to feohgifre
> ne næfre gielpes to georn,   ær he geare cunne.

> 'A wise man should be patient;
> neither should he be too hot of heart nor too hasty in speech,
> neither too wanting in courage nor too reckless,
> too fearful nor too joyful nor too covetous
> nor too prone to the boast e'er he knows himself well.'

It should be noted that Wulfstan is considerably later than the date usually given for the composition of *The Wanderer*, but Suddaby suggests that the Wulfstan and *Wanderer* passages are both based on an early gnomic tradition.

Such source study is interesting and to a point significant; how-

---

[20] Susie I. Tucker, "Return to *The Wanderer*", *EIC*, VIII (1958), 229.
[21] Elizabeth Suddaby, "Three Notes on Old English Texts", *MLN*, LXIX (1954), 465.

ever, it has the troublesome shortcoming of overlooking completely the relevance of the lines to the development of the theme.
What is important to the poem as a whole is that the generalizations which make up the passage follow with unassailable logic the
lines immediately preceding it in which the wanderer has cited the
wisdom found in experience, and that they continue the development of the eschatological motif. The wanderer has already told
us that he is no longer depressed by the evidence around him of
the decay of the world. He next tells us that with the years has
come wisdom and acceptance, moderation and the contemplative
attitude, rather than the impulsiveness of youth. Then at line 73
we begin a long eschatological passage – scenes of general destruction which follow the generalization by the wanderer of his own
personal situation.

The eschatological images of lines 73-87 are an enlargement
upon the images of lines 60-63, in which the wanderer thinks upon
the decay of the world and upon the life of the earls who have
gone so suddenly from the deserted halls. In the later lines he can
and does think deeply and more meaningfully about what God has
promised. A man must think about these things, he seems to say,
in order to make himself ready for the end when it comes. The
stark desolation pictured in the lines also serves to strengthen the
significance of the consolatory lines with which the poem ends.

There is one especially troublesome passage at lines 78b-82a:

                    waldend licgað
dreame bidrorene,   duguþ eal gecrong,
wlonc bi wealle.   Sume wig fornom,
ferede in forðwege,   sumne fugel oþbær
ofer heanne holm.

                'masters lie,
deprived of joy; warriors all have fallen
in pride before the wall. War took some,
carried them far hence; one a bird bore away
over the high sea.'

There is an interesting possible double level of meaning here in
the image of the dead masters. The connection between the prince
and Christ has already been suggested, as has the connection be-

tween the crucifixion and baptism. The dead masters, because of the plural form, may serve as a reminder to the wanderer not only of lost comitatus lords but also of his crucified Lord and thus carry forward the allegorical theme. The second image which attracts attention has, to my knowledge, never been successfully dealt with. This is the image of the bird which carries off the warrior over the sea. Most critics have interpreted the word *fugel* literally and have avoided the problem. However, no less than three figurative interpretations are possible. The word might possibly refer to the Walkyries, since these spirits are known to have assumed bird shapes. The Walkyries, however, appear nowhere else in Old English poetry, and to my knowledge, no one has suggested this interpretation. Another possibility is suggested by Salmon's paper in which she conjectured that the images the wanderer sees in lines 50-55 are the bird-souls of his companions. It is possible that the same interpretation could be put upon the bird figure at this point – the bird spirit's presence at the scene of battle in order to accompany the soul of the slain warrior to its destination beyond the sea. I see one other possibility, an interpretation which has the advantage of being grounded solidly in Old English poetic techniques. The interpretation involves the well-established kenning for the ship as the sea-bird or the ring-necked floater. Many of the Viking and Old English ships had prows which carried bird likenesses, and the kenning was a natural result. May not the line refer to a ship, and in so doing, refer to the literal fact of a warrior's having been carried away as a prisoner? It is true that men were seldom taken captive in the comitatus society, but warriors as hostages are not unknown, as we can see from the 755 entry of the *Anglo-Saxon Chronicle*. The interpretation is strengthened by the fact that the 'bird' is said to have carried the warrior away *ofer heanne holm* 'over the high sea'. Such a reading recalls the inevitable hard lot of the exile.

The well-known *ubi sunt* passage begins with line 88. Here we have the third use of the motif of the wise man, which we have seen previously at lines 65b and 73. The passage strikes the elegiac note in order to give us the full impact upon the mind of the exile of his hard-earned knowledge. The theme of human sadness over the passing of life and the theme of the necessary acceptance of God's Providence both culminate at this point, reaching a climax at line 107 in the repetition of the idea that man's lot is inevitable, *onwendeð wyrda gesceaft weoruld under heofonum* 'the decree of fate changes the world under the heavens'. The use of the word *wyrda* here makes an important parallel with the use of the word at line 5b. The statement at the end of the poem emphasizes the exile's growing wisdom. Its linking of fate (Providence) with both heaven and earth implies the wanderer's full grasp of his situation on both the material and spiritual levels of his existence. The statement in the opening lines, *wyrd bið ful araed*, is, on the other hand, the very essence of despair over the lot which God has cast for His human creature. The statement at line 107 seems to ring with a kind of exultance in the full knowledge of the presence of God's beneficent hand, an expression of the faith that produces wisdom in the face of the hardships a human must endure in order to assure his salvation.

Lines 108-10 contain an important step in the theme of developing wisdom:

> Her bið feoh læne,   her bið freond læne,
> her bið mon læne,   her bið mæg læne,
> eal þis eorþan gesteal   idel weorþeð!

> 'Here goods are fleeting, here friends are fleeting,
> here man is fleeting, here woman is fleeting;
> all this substantial earth becomes empty!'

These lines are a summary statement of the elegiac theme, but they are here so introduced into the structure of the poem that they become not a statement of hopelessness but of hope. The point is that with the wanderer's wisdom has come the recognition that the frailty of earthly things is essentially unimportant. This interpretation is strengthened by the fact that the consolatory passage beginning "so spoke the wise in spirit" follows immediately. It is in this passage that the wanderer reaches his final conclusion that it is well for a man to place his faith in God where all true strength lies.

The theme of the poem develops as follows: a man who is solitary, conscious only of his own hard lot, aware of the hardships of others only through a comparison of their state with his own, prays in despair for the mercy of God. As he prays, and in praying begins to contemplate his situation, he becomes aware that his self-pity is ignoble and unworthy of a creature of God, that, actually, it is a sin and will, therefore, afford neither him nor anyone else help. As this awareness dawns upon him, he recalls the death of Christ and his own participation in that death through baptism. With the thought of baptism comes the memory of the obligation he accepted with baptism to see himself as an exile, a descendant of Adam. Then comes the first real turning point in his awareness, his realization that all worldly pleasure passes but that when his thoughts turn back to his Prince he is no longer depressed by the human lot. With this realization comes the full awareness of, not only what it means to be a *peregrinus pro amore Dei*, but also what God's promise of destruction as well as of redemption means. Only then can come his final acceptance of the inevitableness of God's Providence and his realization that only in the strength of God can man find solace in his exile.

There is a tendency among some scholars to discount the existence of allegory or symbolism as a method in medieval poetry. One such scholar cites *The Wanderer*, saying that the poet does not bring the allegorical figures to the surface and that symbolism would not have been used at so early a date without being fully expounded.[22] Such an argument misunderstands completely the nature of medieval allegory. In the first place medieval allegory was more an appeal to reason than to the senses. Since reasonable thought was so exclusively defined by its adherence to established doctrine, reason itself was subject to rigorous limitation. Further, the relationship between reason and doctrine was governed by strict adherence of literary study to the implications of St. Augustine's theory of words as cortex and nucleus. Such a theory of language demands that the literal language be the vehicle for the allegory, if not the allegory iteself. There was no need for a medieval poet to bring his figures to the surface – they were the surface. Any

[22] I. L. Gordon, "Traditional Themes in *The Wanderer* and *The Seafarer*", p. 12.

medieval man who could read knew that to start with. As to the necessity of expounding symbolism, we may answer this argument in much the same way, since symbolism and allegory were to the medieval mind all but synonymous. Dante's technique in *The Divine Comedy*, where the characters are both allegory and symbol, may be used to represent the medieval method in general. I think it not unfair to say that the poet of *The Wanderer* conceived his characters in much the same symbolic and allegorical context as Dante did his. In both poems the characters give body and human meaning to the allegory and create symbolic overtones. In the Old English poem the wanderer is a real man in a real situation; he suffers cold and hunger and loneliness, but on the symbolic-allegorical level the cold and hunger and loneliness are signs of other relevances on different contextual levels.

Both from internal evidence and from a consideration of the poem in its cultural and historical setting, I find it reasonable to conclude that its theme is Christian and that it is a part of the tradition of Christian lyric elegy which had begun several centuries earlier on the continent.

IV

THE SEAFARER

As in the case of *The Wanderer*, there is general agreement among scholars that *The Seafarer* was composed sometime during the eighth century, at a time during which England's libraries and schools were known throughout the western world and when the Christian church had assumed a dominating role in the culture of the island.

It is generally agreed that *The Seafarer* presents more problems both in theme and structure than does *The Wanderer*. Boer, with his suggestion that lines 58-87 of *The Wanderer* are an interpolation, is the only scholar to question seriously the authenticity of any part of the manuscript material of that poem other than the opening and closing lines.[1] The problem with *The Seafarer* is not so simple. There is still no final agreement concerning the three major questions which have baffled scholarship on the poem for the past century: (1) the question of whether or not there should be a division of the poem and just what will constitute the basis for division; (2) the function of the word *forþon* in the structure of the poem, and (3) the nature of and the seafarer's attitude toward the sea journey which he describes beginning at line 33b.

The poem as we have it appears on folios 81a-83b of *The Exeter Book* and is generally accepted as being 124 lines long. It has usually been divided into two parts at line 64a. The section beginning at line 64b presents some extremely difficult problems in translation and appears to contain passages garbled through scribal transmission, and, toward the end, some omissions.[2] There

---

[1]   R. C. Boer, "Wanderer und Seefahrer", *ZfdP*, XXXV (1903), 6.
[2]   For an interesting conjecture concerning the condition of the manuscript

are two possibly omitted lines in the first part, at lines 16b and 25.[3]

Friedrich Kluge, in 1883, was the first scholar to suggest that lines 64b-end be considered a later homiletic addition.[4] His suggestion still commands a respectable following.[5] Kluge went further, however, than suggesting that the lines were not part of the original poem; he also suggested that the final section was the work of two different men. This idea has not met with the same acceptance as his first. Kershaw and Williams come to a slightly different conclusion, finding a continuity in the sequence of thought as far as line 102.[6] In this contention they are aligned with Benjamin Thorpe's original suggestion that a new piece begins at line 103 and with Lawrence's later acceptance of this possibility. Lawrence pointed out that line 103 begins a new leaf in the manuscript, folio 83a, which fact, he says, "increases the possibility that its contents have no connection with the preceding lines".[7] Lawrence finds a marked pervasive degeneration in the poem after line 103. Williams' conclusion is somewhat baffling since she sees "no definite boundaries" before line 103, yet says that lines 64-end are moralizing and more or less tedious and "sufficiently separated from Part I to deserve a distinct caption".[8]

In 1869 Max Rieger concluded that the entire poem was a dialogue between an old experienced sailor and a young man who desires a life at sea. He divided the poem into seven speeches of varying lengths, four for the old sailor and three for the young

---

following line 64a, see Robert D. Stevick, "The Text and Composition of The Seafarer", *PMLA*, LXXX (1965), 332-336.

[3] Krapp and Dobbie, *The Exeter Book*, Vol. III of *The Anglo-Saxon Poetic Records*, do not agree with the lacuna at line 25b.

[4] Kluge, "Zu altenglischen Dichtungen: I. Der Seefahrer", *Engl. Stud.*, VI (1883), 322-327.

[5] See Wardale, *Chapters on Old English Literature*, p. 61. G. K. Anderson, *The Literature of the Anglo-Saxons*, p. 161, is less insistent. W. W. Lawrence, "The Wanderer and The Seafarer", *JGP*, IV (1902), 460-480, also accepts the final section as a later addition. See also Williams, *Gnomic Poetry in Anglo-Saxon* (New York, 1914), p. 48.

[6] Kershaw, pp. 18-19; Williams, pp. 47-49.

[7] Lawrence, p. 471.

[8] Williams, p. 48.

man.[9] Kluge accepted the dialogue theory but argued that there should be only two speeches, one each for the old sailor and the young man. Since he dropped lines 64b-end from consideration, his theory fitted neatly the two contradictory attitudes toward the sea found in the first 64-½ lines. Boer concluded that the poem was a composite made up of three separate poems. He first isolated lines 1-24 as a fragment of a poem to which he gave the name *The Complaint of the Seafarer;* then, translating *forþon* (line 27) as *darum*, proceeded to one of the crucial passages at line 33b and said that it was illogical for a man to describe the terrors of the sea and then immediately afterward say that he *therefore* desires a sea journey. On the basis of this argument, he concluded that an entirely new poem begins at line 33b. He agreed with Kluge that lines 64b-end were a later homiletic addition but then confounded confusion by accepting Rieger's dialogue theory with the qualification that he could not make up his mind as to whether two men were talking or one man was talking with himself. Lawrence attacked Boer and categorically rejected the dialogue theory on the grounds that it was not natural that a poem of the period would contain dialogue without indicating it. He explained the apparent contradictions in attitude toward the sea by finding them to be conflicting emotions in the mind of one man. Boer had hinted at this possibility. The idea was attacked by Schücking,[10] but was defended by E. Blackman.[11] Ehrismann's suggestion in 1909 that the first 64-½ lines of the poem are an allegory is the conclusion which has since gained the greatest following. O. S. Anderson, Robertson, Smithers, and Huppé have started with Ehrismann's suggestion and have pursued interpretations of the poem in relation to its historical-cultural setting. Ehrismann suggested that the dangerous voyage represented the afflictions of life and also that the life on land represented the materialistic life. The life at sea, he said, represented the monkish life, which considered worldly

[9] Max Rieger, "Der Seefahrer als Dialog hergestehlt", *ZfdP*, I (1869), 334-339.
[10] L. L. Schücking, rev. of E. Sieper, *Die altenglische Elegie*, *Engl. Stud.*, LI (1917), 107.
[11] E. Blackman, rev. of O. S. Anderson, *The Seafarer: An Interpretation*, *MLR*, XXXIV (1939), 254-255.

pleasures sinful. He thought of the entire 124 lines as unified by a pervading homiletic quality. Whitelock attacked the allegorical interpretation in 1950.[12] She had been preceded in this line of thinking by C. L. Wrenn and S. B. Liljegren.[13] Whitelock suggested the literal interpretation of the seafarer as a *peregrinus* of the British or Irish church who chose to find salvation by volunteering himself for dangerous missionary work among foreign lands. In the same year, however, Robertson published his study of *The Wanderer* as allegory. His approach has been followed by Smithers and Huppé. There is further substantiation of the allegorical approach in the work of E. G. Stanley on poetic diction in Old English poetry.[14] Stanley argues that the modern reader makes the mistake of attempting to separate the factual from the allegorical in reading the Old English poems, an attempt which would never have occurred to a man of the early Middle Ages, especially when he was dealing with didactic writing. He further points out that practically all of Old English poetry is didactic. Particularly in non-biblical didactic poems, he says, the didactic purpose came first and bodied forth the fact. In the poetry, he says, suitable facts were introduced to enshroud the doctrine just as the body enshrouds the soul. We may compare Stanley's approach with that of Robertson in the light of the latter's comments upon the 'cortex' and 'nucleus' of a piece of writing which the early medieval reader was trained to look for.

Attempts to pin down the meaning of *forþon* have been almost as equally varied and contradictory as have been the attempts to reconcile the two sections of the poem. Rieger suggested translation as an adversative, 'and yet', or 'but'. Marjorie Daunt, in 1918,

[12] Dorothy Whitelock, "The Interpretation of 'The Seafarer'", *The Early Cultures of North-West Europe*, eds. Sir Cyril Fox and Bruce Dickins (Cambridge, 1950), 268-272.
[13] C. L. Wrenn, *The Year's Work in English Studies*, XIX (1938), 48, and S. B. Liljegren, "Some notes on the Old English Poem *The Seafarer*", *Stud. Neophil.*, XIV (1941-1942), 145-159. See Wrenn's elaboration of his stand regarding the poem in his *A Study of Old English Literature* (London, 1967), pp. 144ff.
[14] E. G. Stanley, "Old English Poetic Diction and the Interpretation of The Wanderer, The Seafarer, and The Penitent's Prayer", *Anglia*, LXIII (1955), 413-466.

defended this translation, arguing that *forþon* is historically an adversative in Germanic languages.[15] Kluge attacked this idea, taking the opposite view, that there is no linguistic justification for translation as an adversative. Daunt pointed out further in her argument that in the Vercelli Homilies the word is translated as meaning 'in spite of' and that in King Alfred's translation of Gregory's *Cura Pastoralis* the word *sed* is translated *forþæm*. Boer generally translates the word *darum*. Lawrence warned against such an exclusive reading, arguing that *The Seafarer* originated in a northern dialect where there is historical evidence for translation of the word as a loose logical connective much like the Modern English 'so'. He further pointed out that *soþlice* appears in many southern manuscripts where in similar passages northern manuscripts have *forþon*. Kershaw in effect dismissed the whole problem by arguing that the word is simply a loose adverbial connective which does not necessarily imply logical connection between the thoughts it joins. She suggests 'I assure thee' or 'assuredly'. Her argument agrees with that of Lawrence.

The third major question, that of the nature of the sea journey and of the seafarer's attitude toward it, has attracted wide attention. In 1951 Greenfield offered a variation on the opinions of Ehrismann, O. S. Anderson, and Whitelock. In his 1965 *A Critical History of Old English Literature* he has considerably altered his earlier conclusions.[16] O. S. Anderson, in 1937, saw no problem in the change in attitude on the part of the seafarer, interpreting the change allegorically as an expression of the seafarer's longing for eternal peace.[17] Greenfield had earlier accepted Whitelock's literal *peregrinus* theory but insisted that the emotional complexity of the poem lay in seeing a pattern of changing attitudes throughout, in the first 64-½ lines from eagerness to trepidation, and in the final 59-½ lines from acceptance of the ascetic ideal to nostalgia for a vanished order. His later interpretation sees the first 64-½ lines as either a literal *peregrinatio pro amore Dei* or an allegory of man's

[15] Marjorie Daunt, "Some Difficulties of 'The Seafarer' Reconsidered", *MLR*, XIII (1918), 474-479.
[16] Greenfield, "Attitudes and Values in 'The Seafarer'", *SP*, LI (1954), 15-20, and his *Critical History of Old English Literature*, pp. 219-220.
[17] O. S. Anderson, *The Seafarer: An Interpretation* (Lund, 1937).

passage to his heavenly *patria* and the final 59-½ lines as an essentially eschatological statement on the necessity of the seafarer's recognizing of his true home in heaven.

My attitudes toward the three problems may be summarized as follows. I believe that the entire poem as it appears in *The Exeter Book* is Christian in theme and structure; I do not think that sufficient evidence exists to warrant discarding any of the manuscript material. I believe that the sea images in the first 30 lines constitute an allegory of human life, but I see no shift of attitude in lines 31-64a, as does O. S. Anderson. I follow him in subdividing the first section of the poem which contains the sea images. I do not hold exclusively with Whitelock's literal reading although I believe that the literal figure of the *peregrinus* is central to an allegorical interpretation of the poem. Finally, I think that the usual translation of *forþon* as 'therefore' suffices in almost every instance in the poem, although I see no reason why the word cannot be used in the sense of a loose adverbial connective in contexts which will not justify the translation as 'therefore'.

The most significant aspect of the seafarer's opening description of his situation is the sense his statement gives of being bound inexorably to, almost imprisoned in, the ship, of being committed without hope of escape to the unpredictable sea. His implication later at lines 33-38 that he welcomes such a life is what has confused so many scholars, but when we read his situation as one in which he has made the Christian's choice of the hard lot of those who seek salvation in a hostile world, the contradiction disappears.

The very first line of the poem, *Mæg ic be me sylfum soðgied wrecan*, suggests the exile theme. The key meaning, regularly overlooked, is in the word *wrecan* 'to drive out', or 'drive on', 'to send', 'to wreak', 'to punish'. The exclusive application to driving out of words I find questionable, although figuratively the meaning is defensible. What is overlooked is the obvious similarity of the form and its meaning to *wrecca* 'an exile', and various related words. Although literal translation of *wrecan* as a verb demands the translation 'I can tell of myself a true tale', the pun on the word also demands, I think, a reading something like, 'I can tell of myself a true tale of exile'. However, if *wrecan* can be read as a variant spelling of *wreccan,* we have a different situation. *Wrecca* is a masculine noun of the weak declension, hence *wreccan* (*wrecan*) is a genetive singular and the literal translation of the line, followed by line 2a, in which *secgan* appropriately fills the syntactic slot which would otherwise have been filled repetitiously by *wrecan,* would be 'I can of myself a true tale of exile, / experiences tell', which reading seems to me the intended one. Such a reading is strengthened by the fact that *gid* (*soðgied*) can signify 'sermon', 'proverb', or 'riddle'.

The opening lines develop the theme of hardship in the life of the exile by placing emphasis upon such aspects of the seafarer's condition as anxiety, watchfulness (expectation), binding fetters, weariness, and inner hunger. Many scholars, such as I. L. Gordon, have said that the audience would have been captivated by the literal realism of the comitatus exile, but such a suggestion fails to take into consideration the religious conditioning to which the early Christian audience was subjected. The fact is, as Stanley pointed out, that such an audience would have taken the realism as an intensifying device to give more impact to the allegory.

The opening 11-½ lines of the poem contain several of the above mentioned images which deserve detailed comment:

> Mæg ic be me sylfum   soðgied wrecan,
> siþas secgan,   hu ic geswincdagum
> earfoðhwile   oft þrowade,
> bitre breostceare   gebiden hæbbe,
> gecunnad in ceole   cearselda fela,
> atol yþa gewealc,   þær mec oft bigeat
> nearo nihtwaco   æt nacan stefnan,
> þonne he be clifum cnossað.   Calde geþrungen
> wæron mine fet,   forste gebunden,
> caldum clommum,   þær þa ceare seofedun
> hat ymb heortan;   hungor innan slat
> merewerges mod.

> 'I can tell of myself a true tale of exile,
> journeyings, how I often endured days of misery,
> times of distress; how I have borne bitter sorrow
> in my keel, have known places of sorrow, where
> fell to me the lot of the hard nightwatch at the
> prow of the boat, when the hostile rolling of

the waves tossed it near the cliffs. My feet were
pinched by cold, bound by frost, by cold fetters.
There the lament of misery was hot around my heart;
an inner hunger set upon the mind of the seaweary.'

The first line has already been commented on. The lines immediately following describe in detail the condition of the seafarer as
he is cast about by the wintry sea, barely avoiding destruction on
the rocky cliffs, palled in the darkness of night. Such a situation,
emphasizing so heavily the weariness, anxiety, and fear of the man,
seems unavoidably to suggest levels of meaning above the literal.
The images in the succeeding lines (8b-12a) present him as
'pinched', 'bound', and 'fettered', images which seem part of a cres-
cendo passage moving toward a climactic statement. Let us consider
just how the seafarer is bound. He is bound by cold fetters, he is
bound by the sea, he is bound to the boat, and perhaps most important, he is bound by an inner hunger. The cold fetters, to be
sure, are not to be taken solely literally, but as figures representing the sea and the cold of winter, perhaps even the inner hunger.
Use of the sea in patristic writing to represent life has been mentioned, but it can also represent the sin of Adam, hence is a fetter,
binding man to a life the end of which is unpredictable. The boat
is a more hopeful image when we realize that in exegetical tradition
boats were often interpreted as the church. The seafarer may be
bound to the unpredictableness of life but he has the assurance of
the church to buoy him until such time as he can learn through
faith the nature of his destiny. The phrase 'inner hunger' at line 11b
has been consistently misinterpreted, it seems to me. The hunger is
usually interpreted as physical hunger. W. S. Mackie gives "and
hunger tormented my soul / till I was weary of the sea".[18] R. K.
Gordon reads, "hunger within rent the mind of the sea-weary
man".[19] Kennedy gives, "Hunger sapped a sea-weary spirit".[20]
O. S. Anderson gives, "hunger within tore / the spirit of the one
weary with roaming the sea".[21] Only Gordon and Anderson give

[18] W. S. Mackie, *The Exeter Book*, Pt. II (= *EETS*, O.S. 194) (London,
1934), p. 3.
[19] R. K. Gordon, *Anglo-Saxon Poetry*, p. 84.
[20] Kennedy, *An Anthology of Old English Poetry*, p. 19.
[21] O. S. Anderson, *The Seafarer: An Interpretation*, p. 34.

the notion of *inner* hunger, but neither develops the idea in his
translation. They leave the lines slightly ambiguous. The poet's inclusion of the word *innan* leaves little doubt that in the context of
the ideas developed in the lines he must have meant the phrase
hungor innan to mean something like 'spiritual desire' or 'anxiety'.
The Christian exile was always conscious of the paradise he had
lost and desirous of regaining it. Not only this, but he was also
aware, as we have seen in the case of the wanderer, of the close
connection between the beginning of his pilgrimage (baptism) and
the death of Christ, his Lord. It is to be noted in this connection
that we do not have in *The Seafarer* the same emphasis upon the
comitatus situation that we had in *The Wanderer*. The contrast between sea and land life gives us a different thematic structure.

Lines 12b-26 establish the fundamental contrast between the
conditions of the land dweller and the seafarer:

>   Þæt se mon ne wat
> þe him on foldan   fægrost limpeð,
> hu ic earmcearig   iscealdne sæ
> winter wunade   wræccan lastum,
> winemægum bidroren   . . .
> bihongen hrimgicelum;   hægl scurum fleag.
> Þær ic ne gehyrde   butan hlimman sæ,
> iscaldne wæg.   Hwilum ylfete song
> dyde ic me to gomene,   ganetes hleoþor
> ond huilpan sweg   fore hleahtor wera,
> mæw singende   fore medodrince.
> Stormas þær stanclifu beotan,   þær him stearn oncwæð
> isigfeþera;   ful oft þæt earn bigeal,
> urigfeþra;   ne ænig hleomæga
> feasceaftig ferð   frefran meahte.

>   'The man who lives on land
> does not understand that, he with whom the fairest abides,
> how I, full of sorrow, abode the winter
> on the ice-cold sea, the path of the exile,
> deprived of loving kinsmen,
> hung about with icicles; hail flew in showers.
> There I heard naught but the sounding sea,
> the ice-cold waves. Sometimes I had the song of the swan
> to give me joy, the gannet's cry,
> the song of the curlew, in place of the laughter of men;

the mew's singing replaced the mead drinking.
Then storms beat upon the stone cliffs, where the
icy-feathered eagle answered, full oft the wet-feathered
eagle screamed. By no beloved kinsmen
might this naked journey be consoled.'

The reference in lines 12b-13 to the man living comfortably on
land is brief but it serves to introduce the theme of the poem. This
contrast and the seafarer's attitude toward it have occasioned most
of the misunderstanding of the poem's structure. The image of the
land man is at the heart of the early arguments for composite structure, the dialogue theories, the disagreement between those who
favor either the allegorical-symbolic or the literal interpretation,
and it has led to the disagreements over whether or not there is
envy or contempt in the reference to the land man, or whether any
attitude at all is expressed. Ehrismann and O. S. Anderson seem
to have come closest to a valid interpretation of the situation;
however, even they do not attribute to the contrast what seems to
me its true significance. Cecil Wood has made what may be a
useful suggestion in this connection.[22] Although what he says cannot be applied specifically to the passage in *The Seafarer,* the
general relevance of his idea to Germanic culture may have a
bearing on our problem. Wood points to a number of Old Norse
sources which make a distinction between those men who take an
active part in life and those who do not. He finds that the references
to those who avoid physical activity are for the most part filthily
insulting. The contempt with which such men were held is obvious,
Wood concludes. He suggests that this attitude is an inheritance
from a purely Germanic tradition. If his conjecture is a valid one,
and the number of instances he finds in the literature is convincing,
his conclusion gives strength to my suggestion that there is a
definite note of contempt developed throughout *The Seafarer* for
the man who remains on land and avoids participating actively in
life's challenges. In the allegorical application, the man comfortable on land is the man who has shirked his duty as a Christian
exile, a duty of which he is surely aware, and as such is to be contrasted with the seafarer adrift on the stormy sea. The lines fol-

[22] Cecil Wood, "Nis Þæt Seldguma", *PMLA*, LXXV (1960), 481-484.

lowing the introduction of the land-dweller develop the contrast between the moral commitments of the two types of men. The final lines of the poem make the 'application' of the situation described allegorically in the first section. Lines 16, 21, 22, 25, 41, and 43 make possible references to the comitatus background of the seafarer. Only in lines 16, 21, and 22 does the seafarer directly associate himself with the meadhall and even here, since the reference must be taken in the context of the seafarer-land-dweller contrast, we may have a figurative use of the idea. Line 25, half of which is apparently missing, seems to be a general intensive. Line 41 is part of a generalization upon the condition of the exile, not a specific reference to this particular man, and line 43 is now generally considered to be a reference to Godhead. References to prince and treasure which occur in the homiletic passage are not only general but must be taken as part of the homiletic context. The nature of the references does not seem adequate grounds for insisting on a literal reading of the poem.

The second introduction of the land-dweller comes at line 27 and is about twice as long as the previous one:

> Forþon him gelyfeð lyt, se þe ah lifes wyn
> gebiden in burgum, bealosiþa hwon,
> wlonc ond wingal, hu ic werig oft
> in brimlade bidan sceolde.
> Nap nihtscua, norþan sniwde,
> hrim hrusan bond, hægl feol on eorþan,
> corna caldast. Forþon cnyssað nu
> heortan geþohtas, þæt ic hean streamas,
> sealtyþa gelac sylf cunnige.

> 'Therefore, to him it means little, he who has life's joys,
> ensconced in cities with little of misfortune,
> proud and flushed with wine, how I, weary, always
> must remain on the sea-path.
> Night shade darkened, snow fell from the north,
> frost held the land, hail fell upon the earth,
> coldest of grain. Therefore, thoughts now
> press upon my heart that I myself the high seas,
> the salt wave-play will know.' (27-35)

Two words in the passage deserve brief comment, *gelyfeð*, line

27a, and *brimlade*, line 30a. *Gelyfeð* in this syntactic context apparently must be translated 'means', or something similar, but the word also means 'to believe', 'to trust', 'to hope', 'to endear'. Line 30a might well be translated 'Therefore, in him there is little faith', and although the literal context will not bear the translation, I feel sure that the poet meant us to hear the play on the word. *Brimlade*, literally 'sea-path', also has possible overtones. The element *lad* means also 'sustenance', 'provision', 'means of subsistence', and is used in the *Ormulum* with the sense of 'guidance'. Such a second meaning very possibly implies that though the seafarer's situation in the stormy sea is apparently hopeless, he is not without the strength and guidance of his faith.

The phrase *wlonc ond wingal* at line 29a deserves more attention than is usually given it. It is generally passed over as indicating simply that the land man leads a comfortable life. However, I think that much more is intended. The words 'proud and flushed with wine' would certainly suggest to the medieval audience the two cardinal sins of pride and gluttony. The phrase seems a resounding condemnation of the land-dwellers. The condemnation serves as a strong note on which to conclude the first section of the poem, which, as I see it, ends at line 30.

O. S. Anderson suggested a division of the first 64-½ lines at line 33; however, such a division detracts from the strength of the thematic development, whereas a division at line 30 adds to the impact of the allegorical significance of the sea imagery. The division at line 33 attaches the lines describing the darkening night and the snow storm to the immediately preceding lines concerning the final contrast between sea and land life. In the division which I suggest they open the following section, which begins a new treatment of the sea. If it is reasonable to assume that the first 30 lines develop an allegory of the sea as life and emphasize the contrast between the seafarer and the land man as representative of two conflicting commitments to that life, it seems much more effective to close the section with the emphasis on the contrast. To connect lines 31-33a with the first 30 lines creates an abrupt juncture of the images and a resulting obscurity. If, however, lines 31-33a introduce the second stage of the development of the sea image, they set the tone for a deepening of the seafarer's realization of the nature of human experience, his own mortality, and of his voluntary acceptance of his *peregrinatio*. The intensification at this point of the images of darkness and the suggestion in them of terror before the irrevocable might of God and nature anticipate the new development of the sea allegory in lines 33b-71. The images also effect a vivid intensification of the note of elegiac nostalgia which pervades the poem and anticipates the eschatological motif.

This suggested reading of the first section serves another purpose also. It brings into prominence the striking metaphor *hægl feol on eorþan, / corna caldast*. The figure is a vivid one and performs a definite function in the thematic development at this point, a function which seems to have been overlooked, because, I believe, of the association of the lines with the preceding sea imagery. The bringing together in the image of the hail pellets the two diametrically contrasting notions of, on the one hand, life-sustaining grain, with its suggestions of the hot, ripening sun and the fertile earth, and, on the other hand, the killing, sterilizing cold of the hail itself is here particularly apt. The metaphor serves as a perfect transition between the two images of the sea, the images in lines 1-30 representing the life of the exile, and that in lines 31-71 pointing to the inevitable death of all things mortal and to the impending end of the world. The eschatological implications do more, however, than suggest terror before the awful might of God; in their looking forward to the bliss of salvation they suggest the added richness and complexity of the attitude of mind which the Christian *peregrinus* attains as a result of his pilgrimage.

The intensive pronoun *sylf* at line 34b points to the figurative significance of the sea as the journey into death. If read literally, it indicates that the seafarer has not yet been to sea. It cannot, of course, mean that. The confusion that has resulted from such a literal reading can readily be seen in the contradictory attempts of the nineteenth-century scholars and their followers to explain the passage. The pronoun indicates the seafarer's realization that even after the hard life which he has led he still faces, as do all men, seafarers and land-dwellers alike, the final test of death.

The three lines that follow contain two words that present interesting possibilities:

> monaõ modes lust   mæla gehwylce
> ferõ to feran,   þæt ic feor heonan
> elþeodigra   eard gesece.   (36-38)

Elþeodigra, line 37a, has been a constant source of trouble; however, most translators have agreed that it probably refers to some faraway land. They have stuck fairly close to the literal meaning, which tendency, as in the case of *sylf*, has led to considerable disagreement and ambiguity. R. K. Gordon reads the lines, "the desire of the heart always exhorts to venture forth that I may visit the land of strange people far hence".[23] O. S. Anderson reads, "My heart's desire incessantly calls on my spirit / to set forth in search of the land / of another people far from here".[24] Kennedy gives, "Never a day but my heart's desire / Would launch me forth on the long seapath, / Fain of far harbors and foreign shores".[25] Mackie translates, "Heart's desire ever urges / my soul towards departing, that far from here / I should visit the home of strangers".[26] Mackie's reading of *modes* as 'soul' seems the most satisfactory, since it can be taken to imply that the seafarer's journey will be a permanent one. However, the translation of *gesece* as 'visit' does not catch what to me seems to be the meaning of the line. All of these readings seem loath to stray from the safety of a literal translation of *elþeodigra*. The literal reading has the authority of Bosworth-Toller, which gives the adjective *elþeodig* as 'strange, foreign, barbarous', and the noun *elþeodignes* as 'being or living abroad, pilgrimage'. However, there is an interesting use of the word in the Blickling Homily for Quinquagesima Sunday not so far removed in time from the composition of the poem to be of significance:

Forþon we habbaþ nedþearfe þæt we ongyton þa blindnesse ure ælþeodignesse; we send on þisse worlde ælþeodignesse; we synd on þisse worlde ælþeodige, & swa wæron siþþon se æresta ealdor þisses men-

[23] R. K. Gordon, *Anglo-Saxon Poetry*, p. 85.
[24] O. S. Anderson, *The Seafarer: An Interpretation*, p. 35.
[25] Kennedy, *An Anthology of Old English Poetry*, p. 20.
[26] Mackie, *The Exeter Book*, Pt. II, p. 5.

niscan cynnes Godes bebodu abræc; & forþon gylte we wæron on þysne wræc-siþ sende, & nu eft sceolon oþerne eþel secan.

'Therefore it is needful for us to perceive the blindness of our pilgrimage; we are in the foreign land of this world – we are exiles in this world, and so have been ever since the progenitor of the human race brake God's behests, and for that sin we have been sent into this banishment, and now we must seek here-after another kingdom.' [27]

This homiletic use of the word to express an allegorical figure so pervasive in early medieval Christianity would seem to make reasonable the translation of *elþeodigra eard gesece* 'seek the home of the exiles'. Since the home is described as *feor heonan*, we are safe, it seems to me, in assuming that what is being designated here is the Civitate Dei, the Christian's *patria*.

The word *mæla,* as in the readings cited above, is usually translated 'incessantly', 'always', or 'ever', giving a sense of urgency to the lines. Such translation seems to have the authority neither of Bosworth-Toller nor of any tradition of usage. Bosworth-Toller gives, however, a highly interesting usage, 'a mark, sign, cross, crucifix'. Translation of the word as 'sign', especially if we keep in mind the close connection in the allegorical context (strengthened by the Bosworth-Toller entry) of 'sign' with 'cross' or 'crucifix', brings to the lines a clarity which no other translation has been able to bring. Including the translation of *elþeodigra* as suggested, the lines would read:

> 'My spirit's desire is urged by every sign
> to fare forth, that I far hence
> seek the home of the exiles.'

There is another point to be made in defense of the suggested translations of *mæla* and *elþpeodigra*. When these words are so translated, the sense of the entire passage allows the usual translation of *forþon* as 'therefore' at two crucial points, lines 33b and 39. The translation at line 33b has already been defended. Line 39 follows immediately the lines just discussed and draws a conclusion based on the ideas expressed in them:

> Forþon nis þæs modwlonc   mon ofer eorþan,
> ne his gifena þæs god,   ne in geoguþe to þæs hwæt,

[27]   Morris (ed.), *The Blickling Homilies* (London, 1967), pp. 20-23.

ne in his dædum to þæs deor,   ne him his dryhten to þæs

þæt he a his sæfore   sorge næbbe,   hold,
to hwon hine dryhten   gedon wille.

'Therefore is no man on earth so proud of spirit,
nor of his gifts so generous, nor in his youth so vigorous,
nor in his deeds so valiant, not so gracious in the eyes
                                                          of his lord
that he have not anxiety concerning his sea-journey,
as to what his Lord will do with him.'   (39-43)

In line 39a there is a significant echo of a word used earlier.
Modwlonc echoes the phrase *wlonc ond wingal* at line 29a and
thereby strengthens the allegorical interpretation by making lines
39-43 a direct reference to the land-dweller and thus developing
further the contrast between the two attitudes toward life which is
the central theme of the poem.

Greenfield has noted in the poem what seems to him a number
of deliberate plays on words, *doubles entendres,* or puns.[28] He
has noted the play on *dryhten* at lines 41b and 43a, where in the
first instance the word refers to the earthly lord and in the second
to the heavenly Lord. He also points to the word *dreamas* at lines
65a and 86b, where in the first instance the word refers to the joys
of the heavenly kingdom and in the second to the joys of the world.
He also points out plays on words based on similarity of sounds,
such as on *cnossian* at line 8a, the tossing or beating of the ship
near the cliffs, and *cnyssian* at line 33b, etymologically related to
cnossian and referring here to the beating of the heart. Also in this
category he cites *gemonian* at line 50a, referring to the burgeoning
of the fields, and *monian* at line 53a, the two words etymologically
related and the latter referring to the mournful cry of the cuckoo.
In all such instances, the comparisons produce sharply ironic
effects. Greenfield finds that such word-play gives the poem "a
sustained complexity of attitude and diction", but he does not
specify what the attitude is or how the complexity helps to sustain
it. I submit that such word-play bears in every instance on the contrast between the life of the seafarer and the life of the land-
dweller, and, in so doing, further develops the theme of the poem.

[28] Greenfield, "Attitudes and Values in 'The Seafarer'", pp. 18-20

This relationship to the theme is particularly sharp in the *gemonian-monian* pair, *gemonian* suggesting the good life on land, *monian* the sad anxiety of the seafarer as he anticipates his final voyage to the exiles' home far hence. In addition to those pointed out by Greenfield, I find other examples which add to the thematic development.

In the first line of the poem there is the pun on *wrecan*, mentioned earlier. At line 40a there is a possible pun on the word *god:*

> Forþon nis þæs modwlonc   mon ofer eorþan,
> ne his gifena þæs god,   ne in geoguþe to þæs hwæt.

The lines would usually be translated

> 'Therefore is there no man on earth so proud in spirit,
> nor of his gifts so generous, nor in his youth so vigorous'

It is fascinating to entertain the possibility that the poet meant a subtle pun on *god,* which, if the vowel be shortened, means 'God'. Such a pun would constitute a cutting comment on the man who places his faith in the false felicity of earthly goods (the land-dweller). The pun is all the sharper if we note the word *modwlonc* in the preceding line, establishing the comment as one on man's blind pride.

Greenfield has already noted the play on *dryhten* at lines 41b and 43a. There is another play on a form of the word at line 85:

>   Dagas sind gewitene,
> ealle onmedlan   eorþan rices;
> næron nu cyningas   ne caseras
> ne goldgiefan   swylce iu wæron,
> þonne hi mæst mid him   mæþa gefremedon
> ond on dryhtlicestum   dome lifdon.

>   'The days are passed away,
> all the pomps of earth's kingdom;
> there are now neither kings nor emperors
> nor gold-givers, such as were of yore,
> when they, the greatest, performed among themselves glories
> and lived in the most lordly power.'   (80b–85)

As in the previous instances, the pun is at the expense of the man who takes his stand on the side of earthly rather than heavenly glory. *Dryhtlicestum* here may refer to either earthly or spiritual power but, paradoxically, make the same moral comment. Whether the days gone by are those of the greatness of the comitatus society or those of the greatness of the men closest to the life of Christ and the primitive church, the world is seen as now full of men whose ideals have degenerated, of men who live *wlonc ond wingal*. If the emphasis is upon exclusively spiritual meaning, the passage is a cogent reminder of the need for rededication, but even if the meaning is read simply as that applicable to the secular elegy, the context makes it impossible to overlook the eschatological suggestion of the sixth age of the world. The import of the pun is intensified when it is noticed that the lines immediately preceding have been a pointed warning that a cloistered virtue will not do, that active participation in the Christian life is better than calm resignation to the nature of the world.

There is a possible play on the word *strongum* at line 109, *Stieran mon sceal strongum mode, ond þæt on staþelum healdan*. The entire line, as a matter of fact, has never, to my knowledge, been properly translated. R. K. Gordon gives, "One must check a violent mind and control it with firmness".[29] Mackie reads, "One should restrain a stubborn mind and hold it within bounds".[30] But *stieran* means most often 'to steer, guide as a vessel', and *strongum* can as easily mean 'strong' as 'stubborn' or 'violent'. The line should be translated, 'One should hold his course with a strong spirit and keep to that foundation'. Such translation not only establishes a logical transition from the preceding lines which others miss but it also brings the lines that follow into a proper logical sequence: 'One should hold his course with a strong spirit and keep to that foundation, / steadfast to men, pure in manners.'

To return to the second sea image. The development of this image presents us with a crux that has defied all attempts at reconciliation, the suggested break at line 64a. There is still sharp disagreement over whether or not the final 59-½ lines should be included as a part of the poem. Williams in 1914 suggested that the poem was a unit to line 103, basing her conclusion on Thorpe's

29 R. K. Gordon, *Anglo-Saxon Poetry*, p. 86.
30 Mackie, *The Exeter Book*, Pt. II, p. 9.

suggestion that folio 83a was out of place and contained material
not originally intended as a part of *The Seafarer*. Cross has
recently made a suggestion that has come closer to dealing with
the passage. He holds that the descriptive passage which develops
the second sea image ends at line 66a rather than at line 64a and
that the moral application begins at line 66b.[31] His contention
deserves serious consideration.

I have already suggested that lines 39–71 seem to form a unit
which sets the allegorized sea image into a pattern of generalization upon the contrast between sea and land life and to point a
specific warning concerning the fate awaiting those who do not
accept their lot as exiles. If, as I suggest, the sequence of ideas
moves directly through the crux passage without interruption,
there is good reason to believe that no real problem exists. The
sequence of ideas beginning at line 31 runs as follows:

Lines 31–38 – The storms and hardships of mortal life settle
upon the spirit of the seafarer, calling his attention to the fact that
death awaits all pilgrims, in fact, all men whether they be pilgrims
or not.

Lines 39–47 – The necessity of facing death reduces to insignifi-
cance all worldly pursuits, all earthly pride, for no man, neither
seafarer nor land-dweller, can escape anxiety over the inevitability
of death.

Lines 48–55a – Even the burgeoning earth is a reminder that all
that grows dies, and the ironically sad note of the cuckoo warns
that though summer is here winter follows.

Lines 55b–57 – The land-dweller has shut his mind and heart to
the truth about himself and refuses to accept the lessons the world
teaches.

Lines 58–71 – Having learned his lesson well through hardship, and realizing that the land-dweller will not, the seafarer sends
his spirit abroad over the four corners of the earth (accepts completely what his earthly pilgrimage has to teach him) and finds that
the knowledge thus gained makes him even more eager than before to leave the decaying and falling earth and find his true and

---

[31] James E. Cross, "On the Allegory in *The Seafarer* – Illustrative Notes",
MAE, XXVIII (1959), 105.

stable home with his Lord, even though death be the only way, for the joys which God has promised are far more dear to him than the joys promised by this world. The joys of this world decay before his eyes every day through one of three things: illness, old age, or war.

Such a sequence of thought seems to move directly through the crux and to eliminate the problem of the division into parts at line 64a.

At line 72 begins one of the most difficult passages of the poem. A number of possible translations of the lines have been given.

> Forþon þæt bið eorla gehwam   æftercweþendra
> lof lifgendra   lastworda betst,
> þæt he gewyrce,   ær he on weg scyle,
> fremum on foldan   wið feonda niþ,
> deorum dædum   deofle togeanes,
> þæt hine ælda bearn   æfter hergen,
> ond his lof siþþan   lifge mid englum
> awa to ealdre,   ecan lifes blæd,
> dream mid dugeþum.   (72-80a)

R. K. Gordon's reading seems to me to leave the relationship of the tenses confused:

'Wherefore, the praise of living men who shall speak after he is gone, the best of fame after death for every man, is that he should strive ere he must depart, work on earth with bold deeds against the malice of fiends, against the devil, so that the children of men may later exalt him and his praise live afterwards among the angels forever and ever, the joy of life eternal, delight amid angels.'[32]

The translation is at best awkward, although the sense of the poetic passage seems fairly clear: a man should work during his life in order to assure his fame after death and his salvation into the bargain. The good fight against evil will earn both earthly and spiritual rewards. There is a human dimension to these poems as well as a theological, which, if ignored, not only denies the true nature of the medieval allegory but renders them rather two-dimensional. Specifically, the difficulty in all translations of this passage is in the reading of the first two lines, which state the time relationship

[32]   R. K. Gordon, *Anglo-Saxon Poetry*, p. 85.

involved between the acts of the noble men and the praise of those acts. Sisam's reading of the passage is not much smoother than Gordon's even though he leaves out lines 72b–73a:

'So that shall be to each of earls ... the best after fame: that, ere he must away, he bring it about by beneficial actions upon the earth against the malice of fiends, by doughty deeds against the devil, that the sons of men afterward praise him.' [33]

This reading leaves the word "after" ambiguous, although we may guess that the time being suggested is that after earthly life. Mackie comes closest to a good reading:

'So to every man it brings praise from those who live
and speak about him after his death, the best of
                                posthumous fame,
that he succeed, before he must depart,
in prevailing, in this world, against the enmity of fiends
by means of valiant acts against the devil,
so that the sons of men may afterward extol him
and his praise then live among the angels
for ever and ever, the glory of eternal life,
bliss amid the hosts of heaven.' [34]

This translation has the virtue of having straightened out the logical progression of the thoughts, particularly in having distinguished the earthly and heavenly rewards. The translation which I suggest offers what seems to me a further straightening out of this difficult distinction:

'Therefore, it brings praise of the living to each noble man, the best of reputations from those who will speak afterward, that he lay up before he must be on his way benefits on earth against the malice of fiends, by fierce deeds against the devil, that the sons of men shall afterward extol him, add to the praise of his life a life amid angels forever and ever, treasure amid the heavenly host.'

The simplification of the problems involved here allows the lines to find their proper place in the theme of contrast between those who meet their human and Christian obligations and those who do not.

[33]   Kenneth Sisam, "The Seafarer, ll. 72ff", *Engl. Stud.*, XLVI (1912-1913), 336. See also Daunt, " 'The Seafarer', ll. 97-102", *MLR*, XI (1916), 337-338.
[34]   Mackie, *The Exeter Book*, Pt. II, p. 7.

Lines 80 and following bring to a climax the eschatological motif which compares the sixth age of the world with the withering body of an old man. The lines also contain a passage troublesome to translators, lines 94–102. Most editors read lines 94–97 as a complete sentence, thereby isolating it from line 98, which line they consider the heart of the crux. It seems to me, however, that lines 94–97 have a direct connection with the sense of the lines which follow and may, when read together with them, aid in resolving the crux.

> Ne mæg him þonne se flæschoma,   þonne him þæt feorg losað,
> ne swete forswelgan   ne sar gefelan,
> ne hond onhreran   ne mid hyge þencan.
> Þeah þe græf wille   golde stregan
> broþor his geborenum,   byrgan be deadum,
> maþmum mislicum   þæt hine mid wille,
> ne mæg þære sawle   þe biþ synna ful
> gold to geoce   for godes egsan,
> þonne he hit ær hydeð   þenden he her leofað.   (94-102)

It is an interesting phenomenon that most translators agree as to the sense of the lines yet are unable somehow to fit them into the development of the theme at this point. This difficulty seems to me to account for the continued attempts to translate the lines, although none of the translations is markedly different from any of the others. In the following translation, I begin at line 80b and read through line 102:

> 'The days are passed away,
> all the pomps of earth's kingdom;
> there are now neither kings nor emperors
> nor gold-givers, such as were of yore,
> when they, the greatest, performed among themselves glories
> and lived in the most lordly power.
> Vanished is all this host, gone is the glory;
> weak men now live and hold this earth,
> consume it by toil. Glory is cast down;
> the earth's lordliness is old and sear,
> as is also now every man throughout the world;
> old age creeps upon him, he grows pale from want,
> the gray-haired grieves, knowing that his friends of yore,
> the children of princes, are given to the earth.

> Then, when he has lost both body and soul,
> when he can neither swallow sweet nor feel pain,
> nor stir with his hands, nor think with his mind,
> though the grave be strewn with gold
> by his born brothers, though he be buried among the dead
> with great treasure, that will not go with him.
> To the soul full of sin,
> gold which he hoarded while he yet lived here
> will not aid against the sovereignty of God.'

The sense of the lines seems clear enough, and the centrality of the passage to the eschatological motif and to the lines of homiletic admonition which are to follow seems reasonably established. The passage carries forward the theme by continuing the exhortation against the laying up of earthly treasure and the shirking of one's Christian duty. The contrast between seafarer and land-dweller is being elaborated in the homiletic warning.

Lines 103–10 seem also clear enough. Thorpe's suggestion that perhaps a leaf of the manuscript is out of place here, resulting in the intrusion of material not meant to be in the poem, has been mentioned. It seems to me, however, that the sense of the poem proceeds without interruption, particularly if the translation which I have suggested for line 109 be accepted.

The final crux to be dealt with occurs at lines 111–16:

> scyle monna gehwylc   mid gemete healdan
> wiþ leofne ond wið laþne * * * bealo,
> þeah þe he hine wille fyres   fulne * * *
> oþþe on bæle   forbærnedne
> his geworhtne wine.   Wyrd biþ swiþre,
> meotud meahtigra   þonne ænges monnes gehygd.

Most scholars agree that the sense of the lines is that a man should be moderate both in love of friend and hatred of enemy. The exhortation at line 109 that the exile keep to a true course based on faith suggests such moderation and serves therefore as a reasonable introduction to the thought here. Of course, the major difficulty in the lines is the apparent lacunae at lines 111 and 112. Numerous emendations have been suggested, but the state of the text at these points makes virtually impossible any final agreement concerning the lines. The difficulty of dealing with the lines is attested by the fact that R. K. Gordon omits the entire passage from his translation. Malone gives the usual reading to the lines:

> 'Aright each man should rule evil,
> to loved and loathed alike do no wrong,
> though folded in fire he fain would have
> (or burnt on bale to bones and ashes)
> the friend he found! Fate is stronger
> God is greater than the grasp of man.'[35]

Malone's comment on his interpretation is worth quoting in full:

The poet, after laying down the general principle, illustrates it with an extreme case. If one makes a friend, and that friend proves false, so false that one would like to give him pagan rather than Christian burial (in other words, damn him eternally), even then, says the poet, one must do him no wrong.[36]

Although Malone takes some liberties with the translation, his interpretation, I think, is essentially correct. Such a statement by the poet is a fitting conclusion to a theme which has exploited two extreme attitudes toward the question of what constitutes the most meaningful life a man can lead. We have been left in no doubt as to which life either the seafarer or the poet thinks is best. The poem's entire structure has turned on this attitude seen against its contrasting one. So now, as the poet draws his poem to a close and makes ready to give the final homiletic plea, what is more appropriate than a call for moderation and humility on the part of the man who must necessarily be tempted to express some contempt or even feel some envy toward the man *wlonc ond wingal*, even though he knows that the man has placed himself on the road to eternal damnation? It is the fitting climax to the Christian evaluation of the situation. The closing lines, 117–24, are the straightforward exhortation to all men to turn their eyes toward their true heavenly home.

As in the case of *The Wanderer*, both internal evidence and evidence which places the poem in its historical background seem to indicate more than a reasonable possibility that *The Seafarer* can be interpreted validly as a Christian allegorical treatment of the problem of man's acceptance of his fate as an exile, as a descendant of Adam.

---

[35] Kemp Malone, "On Seafarer 111-116", *MAE*, VI (1937), 214.
[36] Malone, "On Seafarer 111-116", p. 215.

V

CAEDMON

The names Caedmon and Cynewulf are the only two which have come down to us from among the pre-Conquest English poets. In the case of neither man do we have a great deal of dependable information, but we know more about Caedmon than about Cynewulf as a result of Bede's recording of the Caedmon story in his *Ecclesiastical History of the English People*. The major remaining unsolved problem in the work of these poets concerns its religious nature. There is no question as to the religious sources of the material upon which the poems are based. They make use of scriptural material, saints' lives, and Christian legend generally. However, some scholars, in spite of the obvious religious nature of the material, still question the presence of religious themes in the poems, themes which both fit them into a meaningful historical, cultural, and literary background and also unify structurally each poem.[1]

The use of Bible story as subject matter for poetry had been known on the continent for four centuries before such matter appeared in England. Commodian, in the middle of the third century, had written *Carmen Apologeticum*, a doctrinal epic poem describing the creation, God's revelation of Himself, the coming of anti-Christ, and the end of the world.[2] The similarity of the

---

[1] See, for instance, E. E. Wardale, *Chapters on Old English Literature*, p. 22.

[2] Described in F. J. E. Raby, *A History of Christian-Latin Poetry*, 2nd ed. (Oxford, 1953), pp. 13ff; Moses Hadas, *A History of Latin Literature* (New York, 1952), p. 442; Teuffels' *History of Roman Literature*, rev. and enlarged by Ludwig Schwabe, trans. by George W. Warr, 2 vols. (London, 1900), II, 284.

situations which produced the work of Commodian and that of Caedmon and Cynewulf is significant. The work of all three writers came at times when churchmen were aware of the need of the faith to establish itself against the influence of older cultures and contemporary heresies and was presumably written for the instruction of the unlearned. Such didactic nature is, of course, common to all medieval literature and in no way detracts from its value as art. Another name assosiated with the Christian epic is that of the Spanish nobleman and priest Juvencus, whose *Evangeliorum Libri IV* was well known to the continent early in the fourth century and in England as early as the late seventh century but certainly by the beginning of the eighth.[3] Alcuin lists Juvencus among the authors of the York Cathedral library. The work of Juvencus tells the story of the gospels, is based primarily on the Gospel of Matthew, and shows definite Virgilian overtones.[4] Again, there is similarity of purpose in Juvencus and the Old English poets. Raby states the case.

Its interest lies in the attempt to provide a Christian literature which might counteract the influence of the pagan poets by showing that the church had her own heroic story, her own epic of the incarnation, the wonderful life, death, and resurrection of the Saviour.[5]

The work of Sedulius was also widely known in England during the late seventh century. He is listed by Alcuin and cited by Bede.[6] His fifth-century *Carmen Paschale* has been called the predecessor of the Old English *Exodus*.[7] Sedulius treated first the miracles of the Old Testament foretelling the coming of Christ, then proceeded to a similar treatment of the miracles of the New Testament, and ended with an account of the Passion, the Resurrection, and the Ascension. The work is a freer treatment of the gospel story than is found in Juvencus and abounds with allegorical treatment of the material characteristic of biblical exegesis and of much Christian

[3] J. D. A. Ogilvy, *Books Known to the English, 597-1066* (Ann Arbor, 1967), p. 190.
[4] Raby, pp. 17ff; Teuffel, II, 324ff; Hadas, pp. 426-427.
[5] Raby, pp. 17-18.
[6] Ogilvy, p. 239.
[7] James W. Bright, "The Relation of the Caedmonian *Exodus* to the Liturgy", *MLN*, XXVII (1912), 101.

poetry of the early Middle Ages.[8] In the fifth century are works
such as the fragmentary *Heptateuchos* of Cyprian, the Gallic poet,
an epic treatment of the Old Testament from Genesis to Judges;
poetic versions of Genesis by Hilary of Arles and Marius Victor;
an epic in five books by Avitus of Vienne covering Old Testament
material from the creation to the crossing of the Red Sea; and Dracontius' version of Genesis in heroic verse.[9]

In addition to these forerunners of the epic treatment of Bible
story, we have at least two well known treatments of the story of
the Cross: the third-century *De Pascha*, an allegory by Marius
Victorinus, and the sixth-century *Pange Lingua gloriosi* of Venan-
tius Fortunatus, both anticipations of the treatment of the Cross
in *The Dream of the Rood* of the Cynewulfian school. The popularity of Fortunatus in England is attested by Ogilvy's research but
knowledge of the work of Victorinus in England remains in dispute.
Alcuin lists a Victorinus in the York Cathedral library but we
cannot be sure which of the many men by that name he meant,
and the *De Pascha* has been attributed to Cyprian and Tertullian
as well as to the elusive Victorinus Poeta.[10]

These are by no means all the works that deal with Bible story
and Christian legend in the same literary genres which we find in
England in the seventh and eighth centuries. To be sure, we cannot prove that all the works mentioned were known in England
during the period of the Old English poetic tradition, but we do
have proof that a majority of them were. The question as to what
books were available to English scholars and poets is far from
settled, and we may reasonably assume from what we know of the
zeal for learning among the English that many more books were
available than we have record of. The library burnings of the
Danes in the late eighth century no doubt destroyed more than we
know.

[8] Raby, pp. 108ff; Teuffel, II, 498ff; Hadas, pp. 431-432.
[9] These works are mentioned in either Raby, Teuffel, or Hadas or in most
standard histories of Latin literature. Cyprian of Gaul, however, seems to
be generally overlooked. Raby mentions him; Teuffel reflects a tendency
to confuse him with the third-century Cyprian, bishop and martyr, of
Africa.
[10] Ogilvy, pp. 140 and 156-157.

It is now generally agreed, although there are still a few dissenting voices, that Bede's story of Caedmon is essentially true. We can accept, at least, that a man named Caedmon lived and worked in the monastery at Whitby and at an advanced age began to compose religious poetry, probably with the help of the more learned brothers of the establishment. Bede tells us that Caedmon not only composed his *Hymn* but that he turned much biblical story to verse. Even if Caedmon did not write all the works recorded in the manuscript that bears his name, he almost certainly did influence the men who did compose them. I shall not involve myself with problems concerning the validity of Bede's story, the authorship of the poems, or the manuscript itself, except in cases where these problems bear directly upon the close analysis of the work. I shall discuss *Exodus* as an allegory of man's acceptance of his life in the world as a Christian exile and of the part which the sacrament of baptism plays in that acceptance. In discussing the poem I shall deal with five thematic motifs: (1) God's covenant with His people, (2) the theme of exile, (3) the nautical imagery, (4) the treasure of the Israelites, and (5) the place in the structure of the poem of the supposed interpolations at lines 362–446, the stories of Noah and of Abraham's offer to sacrifice Isaac.

Since the sacrament of baptism is central to my interpretation of the poem, some discussion of the part water imagery plays is necessary. Baptism is symbolic of man's acceptance of a new life in the church, a new life which lays upon him the heavy duty of his obligation as a *peregrinus* who must undertake a search for salvation in his true home in heaven.[11] The numerous references in preceding chapters to patristic writing which emphasized the idea of exile and associated exile with water in some form make unnecessary here repetitious substantiation. However, a brief word should be said concerning the apparently contradictory significance of water in the context of Christian symbolism. Water can be both destructive and regenerative. It can be both a source of the newness

[11] For discussion of water symbolism, see, for instance, F. W. Dillistone, *Christianity and Symbolism* (London, 1955), pp. 183ff; F. R. Webber, *Church Symbolism*, 2nd ed., rev. (Cleveland, 1938), *passim*; H. Flanders Dunbar, *Symbolism in Medieval Thought* (New York, 1961, rprt. of 1929 ed.), pp. 140-141, 230ff.

of life and of the hard obligations which the acceptance of this newness of life entails. Hence, although, as we have seen in the case of *The Seafarer*, the life at sea is to be preferred to a comfortable and meaningless life on land, it is the more difficult to endure. The promise of a newness of life is not only God's promise to man of the possibility of eternal salvation, it is also God's exacting from man a promise in return that he will endure his mortal existence in such a way as to make him deserving of eternal salvation.

The biblical story of the exodus from Egypt is that of the freeing of the chosen people from bondage, a freeing which depended upon the miraculous intervention of God. It is the story of the hard lot of the Israelites in their generation-long wandering across the unknown deserts of Egypt and Arabia in search of their promised home. It is the story of the covenant made between God and His people. Allegorically, it is the story of God's miraculous intervention to free His people from sin and the devil, and following their acceptance of salvation through faith, of God's subjection of their faith to the test of exile. God's intervention in the life of man and man's acceptance of that intervention meet in the sacrament of baptism, represented symbolically in the Old English poem by the crossing of the Red Sea. The hardships of the Israelites' search for the promised land make the forty years of wandering a symbolic counterpart to the wandering of Adam after his expulsion from the Garden, and Adam as the first *peregrinus* is the progenitor of all Christian exiles. The Mosaic Law as covenant then becomes the counterpart in the allegory of the Law as given to Adam. The apparent contradiction in the fact that God willingly led the Israelites out of Egypt, whereas He had expelled Adam, is reconciled by the fact that, to the Christian, baptism is his participation in the death of Christ, his admission of guilt and his acceptance of that guilt.[12] Such a relationship between the Law of Moses and the crucifixion makes the Mosaic Law applicable as a 'sign' which may be interpreted as the Law of the New Testament, thus making of Moses a Christ figure leading His people according to the Law of God as given to Him.

Gollancz, in 1927, was aware of the exegetical tradition sur-

[12] See p. 70, *supra*.

rounding the exodus, but scholars since his time have been more interested in his suggestions concerning the possible misplacement of passages at the end of the poem. Gollancz called the *Exodus* story an allegory of man's progress from the darkness of sin to the light of divine guidance.[13] Cross and Tucker have found a mid-Lent Sunday sermon of Aelfric which follows the medieval tradition in breaking down the allegorical significance of the major figures as follows:

Egypt: the world
Pharaoh: the devil
Red Sea: baptism
Egyptian host: our sins
Sojourn in the desert: exile
Cloudy-fiery pillar: Christ[14]

Bright in 1912 suggested that *Exodus* was based directly upon a Holy Saturday liturgy designed for the baptism of catechumens, the central symbol of which was the paschal candle in the shape of a cloud-like pillar, repesenting Christ.[15] Bright's idea has never gained wide acceptance. Most scholars agree that the symbols which made up this particular liturgy were certainly well known to the poet but see no reason to assume that he based the poem exclusively on the liturgy. Edward B. Irving, Jr., in a paper published in 1959, some six years later than his edition of the poem, in which he was somewhat reluctant to accept fully the allegorical implications, has admitted that the image of life as a sea journey has an important function in the poem. He finds in 1959 that "an exile like that in *The Wanderer* may appear in the closing lines of the poem".[16] His statement implies that he has come to the conclusion that the Christian theme of exile exists not only in *Exodus* but also in *The Wanderer*.

---

[13] Israel Gollancz, *The Caedmon Manuscript* (London, 1927), p. lxix.
[14] James E. Cross and Susie I. Tucker, "Allegorical Tradition and the Old English Exodus", *Neophil.*, XLIV (1960), 122-123.
[15] Bright, "The Relation of the Caedmonian *Exodus* to the Liturgy", pp. 97-98.
[16] Edward B. Irving, Jr., "On the Dating of the Old English Poems *Genesis* and *Exodus*", *Anglia*, LXXVII (1959), 8 n.

Exodus opens in the traditional manner of most Old English poetry
with what has been called a relic of the minstrel's call for attention.[17]
The device is used here as the opening note of the first major
thematic structure of the poem – God's covenant with His chosen
people.[18] We are told immediately of God's favor to Moses in
giving to him the Law. This theme of God's Law pervades the
entire poem. All other thematic structures touch upon it and add
to it, bringing it always into line with the Christian application.

The poet establishes the convenant theme in the opening lines
by clearly playing upon words. Gollancz noted important plays
upon words, which we shall look at later, in the names of the
campsites and the areas traversed by the Israelites in their flight
from Pharaoh toward the Red Sea. The word play in the opening
lines is equally important, since it sets the tone and theme at the
outset. In the opening three lines

> Hwæt! We feor and neah   gefrigen habað
> ofer middangeard   Moyses domas,
> wræclico wordriht,   wera cneorissum, –
>
> 'Lo! We far and near have learned
> throughout the world the laws of Moses,
> wondrous law to the generations of men, –'

there is a pun on the word *wræclico*. Literally the word may be
translated 'wondrous', but it also means 'wretched, miserable', and
is related to the noun *wrecca* or *wræcca* meaning 'exile, wanderer,
pilgrim'. The pun gives added meaning to the lines by suggesting
that the theme of the poem will have to do not only with the Laws
of Moses but also with man's exile, as that exile is related to the
covenant between God and man. The law of exile is certainly a
law 'to the generations of men', since all men are of the race of
Adam. This sense of the timelessness of the Law of Moses makes
possible the linking of Mosaic and New Testament Law, New
Testament Law being the foretold fulfilment of the older Law. One
further point substantiates the interpretation. The word *wordriht*

[17] Irving (ed.), *The Old English Exodus* (= *Yale Studies in English* 122)
(New Haven, 1953), p. 67.
[18] Robert T. Farrell, "A Reading of O.E. *Exodus*", *RES*, n.s. XX (1969),
401-417, deals with the structure of Moses' laws as showing the Help of God
theme.

is usually translated as a plural in order to make it parallel with *domas*. There is no necessity for such translation. *Wordriht* is a neuter a-declension, in which declension the plural is unchanged. It would seem reasonable to suggest that here the poet intended the singular sense, in order to universalize the idea 'law' and thus establish the theme at the outset of the poem.

Another pun occurs at line 32b with the word *forðwegas*.

> Hæfde he þa geswiðed   soðum cræftum
> and gewurðodne   werodes aldor,
> Faraones feond,   on forðwegas.

> 'He had then with true powers
> strengthened and honored the prince of men,
> the enemy of Pharaoh, for his journies.'

The word *forðwegas* refers to the anticipated journey of the Israelites. However, *forðweg* has a figurative as well as a literal meaning, in that it is used to translate, along with other words, the Latin *obitus* 'death'.[19] Such figurative meaning brings sharply into focus the multiple significance of the journey in question. It has been shown that in both *The Wanderer* and *The Seafarer* the journey strongly implies the journey of life, the end of which is death. Such interpretation is particularly applicable to the Christianized theme in that the acceptance of the inevitableness of death is essential to the Christian's acceptance of the hard lot of the exile. Death, in the divine plan, is man's entry into bliss. It is further to be noted that *forðweg* contains the same qualifying element as the Old English euphemism for death, *forðferan* 'to fare forth'. Both these words imply a journey, and journey to a Christian audience of the Middle Ages would suggest both the journey of the *peregrinus* and the inevitable death at the end of the journey. Indeed, this meaning is still implicit in the symbol of the journey in Christian evangelism. Smithers has commented at length on the meaning of *weg* in *The Seafarer* and *The Wanderer*.[20]

Another word suggesting the allegorical context of the journey

---

[19] Bosworth-Toller.
[20] G. V. Smithers, "The Meaning of 'The Seafarer' and 'The Wanderer'", *MAE*, XXVI (1957), 137ff.

occurs at line 53b, where it is stated that the Egyptians thought to forbid, if God allowed, the journey of the Israelites:

        Swa þæs fæsten dreah   fela missera,
50 ealdwerige,   Egypta folc,
        þæs þe hie wideferð   wyrnan þohton
        on langne lust   gif hie metod lete,
        Moyses magum,   leofes siðes.

    'Thus they suffered deprivation many a half-year,
    Vile of old, the Egyptian people,
    Because they thought to turn aside the far travels
    of the kin of Moses, if the Lord allowed them,
    The long desire of the beloved journey.'

The journey, *leofes siðes*, is at the center of one of the most difficult passages in the poem,[21] but certainly refers to the escape which the Israelites desired. Taken literally, the phrase means only that the Israelites were anxious to free themselves from the oppression under which they had so long suffered. However, what we know of the allegorical tradition, strengthened by the fact of Aelfric's correspondence referred to above, makes us aware of the probable suggestion in the lines of the Christian's desire to be free from sin and the temptations of the world, a freedom which, in the Christian context, can be accomplished only by first accepting the sacramental action of baptism in the church. It is possible to sense in such a desire the beginning of the Christian's revolt against the sins that beset him in the mortal world.[22]

One more pun which bears directly upon the journey theme deserves attention, the use of the word *lifweg* at line 104b:

                        Forð gesawon
    lifes latþeow   lifweg metan.

                    'They saw go before them
    life's leader, measuring out the way of life.'

Some editors have emended *lifweg* to *liftweg*.[23] These lines occur in the description of the breaking of the Israelites' third encamp-

[21] See Irving's note to lines 49-53 on p. 70 of his edition.
[22] Gollancz has noted puns on the names of Israelite campsites along the path of their flight to the Red Sea. See his *The Caedmon Manuscript*, pp. lxxxff. These puns will be dealt with later in the analyses of the passages in which they occur.
[23] See Irving's note, p. 75 of his edition.

ment, at Etham, at which encampment they have been made fully
aware of God's presence by the appearance of the pillars. What
could be more consonant with the theme than the realization, once
God's presence is sure, that the journey they have undertaken is
the 'way of life'? Adding strength to this awakening of the Israelites to the true nature of their journey is the dawn image just six
lines earlier at 98a, *þa ic on morgen gefrægn*. The image appears
in the lines describing the breaking of camp at Etham. The movement from darkness to light is a traditional symbol of the dawning
of awareness; in religious symbolism, it is the coming of the divine
light of God's wisdom. The image characterizes the entire journey
up to this point, which is, to recall Gollancz's words, an allegory
of man's progress from the darkness of sin to the light of divine
guidance. The symbolic dawn not only characterizes the journey
up to this point, it illuminates the theme of the entire poem.

The exile image, which is central to the complete thematic development, and is closely involved with the journey motif, enters the
poem at several significant places, such as at lines 3, 56ff., 104,
137–39, 383, and 533–35, among others. I shall dwell on what
appear to me to be the most significant of these passages. The first
occurrence of the image at line 3 has already been discussed. Another appearance is at lines 137–39, in the passage where the
Israelites have pitched their fourth camp, on the shore of the Red
Sea:

135   Ðær on fyrd hyra   færspell becwom,
      oht inlende.   Egsan stodan,
      wælgryre weroda;   wræcmon gebad
      laðne lastweard,   se ðe him lange ær
      eðelleasum   onnied gescraf,
      wean witum fæst.

        'Drear tidings came there to their camp,
      fear of the Egyptians. They stood in horror,
      in fear of the battle with the host; the exile awaited
      the evil of the pursuer, he who had for so long
      imposed by force upon the homeless ones
      hard and constant punishment.'

The Israelites have arrived at the Red Sea and for the first time
hear rumors of the pursuit of the Egyptians. That the exile image

should enter again at this specific point in the journey seems meaningful. The Israelites have committed themselves to the flight and have completed the first phase of their difficult rejection of Egypt and Pharaoh (the world and the devil). They have received full assurance of the guiding and protecting presence of their God in their journey, an assurance without which it would have been impossible for them, we may assume, to find the strength of faith necessary to the acceptance of the miracle of the Red Sea. Since the analogy of the allegory and sacramental structure of the church has been made, it seems reasonable to suggest that the strengthening of the faith of the Israelites prior to their entrance into the Red Sea may correspond with the effect of catechetical instruction prior to the baptism of catechumens. The children of Israel, having received their necessary strengthening through the instruction given them in the form of the miraculous pillars, would be prepared for the great miracle of the sea which would set them on their way toward their promised land, just as the act of baptism seals the Christian upon his *peregrinatio*. As the Israelites see the sea stretching before them and become aware of the pursuit of the Egyptian host (the devil and his worldly temptations ever in pursuit of the Christian) they are made fearfully aware of the nature of their journey and become starkly cognizant of their situation as exiles. It is at this point that the poet reemphasizes their status by referring to them twice in quick succession as 'exiles'. It is to be noted that here again, as at line 3a, a shift from plural to singular has taken place. At line 3a the shift was involved in a noun phrase and its immediately succeeding appositional phrase. Here the shift takes place in two parallel noun clauses, *Egsan stodan* (3rd pl) at line 136b and *wræcmon gebad* (3rd sg) at line 137b. As at line 3a, the significance of the shift seems generally to have been overlooked. The poet here, again, is universalizing his theme by shifting to the less specific form. The poet's use of *eðelleasum* 'homeless', at line 139a, further strengthens the effect of the exile image.

Another occurrence of the exile image is at line 383 in the story of Abraham and Isaac. It should be noted here that the figure strongly substantiates the arguments of those who, like myself, hold that the stories of Noah and of Abraham and Isaac are a part of the poem's thematic structure.[24]

> 380 Þæt is se Abraham   se him engla god
> naman niwan asceop;   eac þon neah and feor
> halige heapas   in gehyld bebead,
> werþeoda geweald;   he on wræce lifde.

> 'This is the Abraham to whom the God of angels
> gave a new name, and likewise gave, far and near,
> the holy tribes into his keeping,
> power over the people. He lived in exile.'

The important point here is that Abraham did not live in exile until after he had accepted the obligation placed upon him by God. It is only after voluntary acceptance that a man is led onto the road to his salvation.

The story of Abraham's wanderings in no small way resembles the story of the exile of the Israelites and their eventual return to the land promised them in the covenant which God had made with them. In both instances we have men who have committed themselves to the carrying out of an obligation, an obligation which will mean deprivation and separation from their homes. To be sure, treasure and riches are given them as a result of their faith, but allegorically these are the spiritual riches which come to one as a result of his faithfulness to God's covenant.

There is one other point in the story of Abraham's exile which is significant. When Abraham returned to Canaan from Egypt he and Lot were rich men, but they fell into disagreement and chose to part. Abraham allowed Lot the first choice of a dwelling place and Lot chose Sodom for his portion. Abraham followed God's command and continued his exile in the countryside. The story as told in Genesis 13 points up specifically the difference in the choices. The situation produced is one which seems to me strikingly similar to the situation which contrasts the seafarer and the

[24] See, for instance, Irving, in his edition, p. 8; Gollancz, *The Caedmon Manuscript*, pp. lxiiff; Stanley B. Greenfield, *A Critical History of Old English Literature* (New York, 1965), who finds that the poem possesses thematic unity (p. 157) although he calls the Noah and Abraham episodes "a questionable flashback" (p. 154).

land-dweller in the thematic development of *The Seafarer*, a motif
introduced into *Exodus* at lines 80ff. I shall discuss these lines
later in another context. Lot is definitely cast in the role of the
land-dweller who does not understand the miraculous presence of
the Lord.

Finally, there is the passage at lines 533–35, after the Israelites'
emergence from the waters:

<blockquote>

                    Þis is læne dream,
  wommum awyrged,   wreccum alyfed,
  earmra anbid.   Eðellease
535 þysne gystsele   gihðum healdað,
  murnað on mode,   manhus witon
  fæst under foldan,   þær bið fyr and wyrm,
  open ece scræf.

</blockquote>

>   'This earthly glory is fleeting,
> strangled in foulness, alotted to exiles
> abiding in misery. Homeless
> in this inn, they remain in unbearable anxiety,
> mourn in spirit, knowing that hell,
> a pit eternally open, where wait fire and worm,
> stands fast beneath the earth.'

The language is unusually figurative and strong. The passage is
the poet's moral 'application' of the preceding narrative, an application which he feels the necessity of making before putting into
the mouth of Moses the final word concerning God's covenant with
His people, which has been passed down to them from Abraham.
The lines bear striking resemblance to the passage in *The Seafarer*,
64ff., and to *The Wanderer*, 108ff. In *The Seafarer*, the passage
makes a moral application of the imagery of storms at sea and of
the towns and burgeoning fields where *woruld onneteð* 'the world
hastens on' (49b). In *The Wanderer*, the passage makes the moral
application of the preceding *ubi sunt* passage and eschatological
imagery. The exile metaphors which are brought to a cluster-point
in the *Exodus* passage are the traditional ones used in patristic
tracts and biblical exegesis where they indicate the insubstantial-
ness of the human situation on earth: the transience of earthly
glory, life as an exile (homeless man), and the inn house of the
world. The piling up of the traditional figures can have been for

one purpose only, to make the didactic point of the allegory.
The *Exodus* passages at lines 56ff. and 104ff. are suggestions of the exile theme, but will not be dealt with at length. Lines 56ff. are those concerning the strange country of Guðmyrce, toward which their leader led the Israelites upon *enge anpaðas, uncuð gelad* 'anxious lone paths, unknown ways' (58). Lines 104ff. are interesting because of their reference to the Israelites' path of flight as their *lifweg* 'life way'. These passages will be dealt with later.

At line 535b there occurs another interesting and highly significant word play, on *gihðum*, which is a form of *gehþo*, 'care, anxiety'. The literal meaning of the word fits the lines, but there is another word, *gihþa* 'an itch, itching', the close similarity of which to *gehþo* and *gihðum* seems to indicate an etymological relationship. The poet's choice of *gihðum* for this passage is surely intended to add a connotative physical sharpness to the notion of man's remaining in 'unbearable anxiety'.

The next thematic motif to be dealt with is that of life as a sea journey. This aspect of the theme involves the much noticed but little understood nautical imagery in the poem. Patristic writing constantly associates life with the figure of the journey, and associates it frequently with a sea journey. Numerous examples have been cited above. In addition, St. John Chrysostom says,

So we must bring our will to fruition by deeds. We also are sailing on a voyage, not from one land to another, but from earth to heaven.[25]

Also, "We all sail upon the same sea".[26] The association of life with a journey, it should be noted from the start, involves the exile motif. In the allegory, as in the church, the *peregrinus* accepts his exile (journey) as his primary obligation following baptism.

The major nautical images which make up this thematic structure are (1) the description of the flight of the Israelites as a sea journey, (2) the reference to both the protecting cloud at Guðmyrce and the twin guiding pillars at Etham as sails, (3) the description of the Israelites as seamen, and (4) the contrast between seamen and

[25] Saint John Chrysostom, *Commentary on Saint John the Apostle and Evangelist, Homilies 1-47*, trans. Sr. Thomas Aquinas Goggin, *The Fathers of the Church*, 72 vols. (New York, 1947-   ), XXXIII, 10.
[26] Saint John Chrysostom, p. 30.

land men. The mention of the images alone serves to recall similar image patterns in *The Seafarer* and *The Wanderer* and constitutes a strong argument for the belief that all the poems here being dealt with were written to serve the same Christian purpose.

Before proceeding with the discussion of the nautical imagery it will be necessary to deal with two problems, one concerning interpretation, the other concerning the manuscript. The problem of interpretation involves the first appearance of the pillar of cloud which acts as guide and protector to the Israelites on their journey. Specifically, the question concerns just when this pillar appears to the Israelites. A cloud appears at lines 56ff., which lines describe the journey to the borders of the land of Guðmyrce, a land described as lying under a covering cloud. Blackburn mistakenly interprets this cloud covering as the first mention of the pillar, and Gollancz seems to follow his lead.[27] The Book of Exodus 13:21, however, makes it quite clear that the pillars did not appear to the Israelites until they had made their third encampment, at Etham.[28] Although the Bible does not mention the trip along the borders of Guðmyrce, it is clear from the poem that the encampment at Etham comes later, in which case the interpretation of Blackburn and Gollancz would appear to be invalid. The mistake in interpretation has led scholars such as Napier and Gollancz to assume a confusion in the manuscript. Both these men have suggested that a leaf from a previous manuscript (from which manuscript the Junius scribe supposedly copied) had been turned around by mistake, resulting in a misplacement of two sections of the poem, and resulting in a confusion in the introduction of the pillars. Napier and Gollancz argue that it is unreasonable to introduce, first one pillar, then both pillars, then the second pillar alone. They feel that it is more reasonable to assume that the poet would have introduced both, then each separately. The poem, however, does not mention a pillar of cloud at Guðmyrce, it mentions only a *lyfthelm* or 'cloud'. Further, the phrase in which the word appears,

---

[27]   F. A. Blackburn (ed.), *Exodus and Daniel* (Boston, 1907), p. 38; Gollancz, *The Caedmon Manuscript*, pp. lxxxff.
[28]   It is at this point that the manuscript problem overlaps the interpretive problem, as the ensuing discussion will indicate.

lyfthelm beþeaht, seems to make plain the meaning 'covered by a cloud'. This does not sound like a towering pillar; rather, it sounds like a broad, stretching layer of stratus. The Bible story does not mention the pillars before the Etham encampment. The poem is actually following the Bible in its introduction of the pillars at Etham.

Both Napier and Gollancz have suggested rearrangements in order to 'correct' what they interpret as the mistake. More recently, Wardale has agreed that a confusion exists but has made no suggestion as to rearranging the poem.[29] Irving has brought some telling arguments to bear against these suggested changes in the text. He has pointed out that the shifts would involve rearranging the numbered sections in which the poem appears in the manuscript. The fact that the sections are now in proper numerical order indicates that the poem is in an intended order. Most important, he points out that the poem makes sense from line to line as it now stands.[30] Both of these arguments seem strong enough to cast doubt on the conclusions of Napier, Gollancz, and Wardale. The apparently mistaken interpretation of the *lyfthelm* covering Guðmyrce strengthens the doubt. As the discussion proceeds, it will be argued that the introduction of the pillars at Etham fits the poet's allegorical theme in such a way that introduction of them at any other point would be meaningless.

Concerning the itinerary of the journey, Gollancz has noted that patristic tradition is not in agreement as to whether Etham is the second or third encampment.[31] He argues that it is the third and that an encampment at Ramses on the first night is overlooked. To overlook the encampment at Ramses, he says, violates the allegorical significance of the journey usually given to it in patristic writing. He cites the Hebrew etymology cited by St. Ambrose of the word *Ramses* as *commotio turbulenta* and argues that the in-

29 Wardale, *Chapters on Old English Literature*, p. 130.
30 Irving's edition, pp. 4-5.
31 The itinerary of the Israelites is set forth in Exodus, chapters 12 and 13 and allegorically in Numbers, chapter 33. Gollancz's etymology of Ramses is from Saint Ambrose, who bases his interpretation on Genesis 33:17:

> Et jacob venit in Socoth; ubi ædificatio domo et fixis tentoriis, appellavit nomen loci illius Socoth, id est Tabernacula.

terpretation suggests the spiritual tumult of the first revolt of the conscience against sin. *Socoth*, he points out, is interpreted in Hebrew as 'tents', which he holds as suggestive of tabernacles. The tabernacle, he says, suggests man's freeing himself from the more material impediments of mortal life and, further, the recognition of God's sheltering power. From Ramses to Succoth, the path has been a difficult one straight through the desert, suggesting the increasing difficulty of the Christians' exile. It is only after these two symbolic encampments, Gollancz suggests, that the full power of God's guiding light could be made clear to the exiles. And so it is in the biblical story. The pillars make their first appearance at Etham.[32] Irving suggests that the poet simply took the opportunity to describe both pillars as they would henceforward appear. It would seem that the poet first introduced the pillars in their guiding function and that later he introduced their second function, associated with the pillar of fire, that of a threat against those who would disobey Moses, or, symbolically, fail to uphold the covenant made with God through Abraham.

After insisting on the symbolic significance given the itinerary in exegetical tradition, Gollancz makes the completely paradoxical statement that the Old English poet was certainly not aware of any of the symbolic implications of the journey, that his interest was completely taken up with the geographical details of the flight. As I have said before, such statements display what seems to me a complete lack of understanding of the nature of early Christian allegory. The geographical details of the flight were precisely the allegory with which the poet was dealing. The details and the allegory cannot be separated.

The nautical imagery enters the poem at line 81, in the passage describing the covering of cloud which protected the Israelites from the intense heat as they moved northward from the borders of Guðmyrce.

Hæleð wafedon,

drihta gedrymost.   Dægsceades hleo

[32] Martin Noth (*Exodus: A Commentary* [Philadelphia, 1962], p. 109), holds that the pillars appeared before Etham, that they led the Israelites to Etham, and that they stand "as a preliminary indication of the whole of the divine guidance of Israel in the wilderness".

80 wand ofer wolcnum;   hæfde witig god
sunnan siðfæt   segle ofertolden,
swa þa mæstrapas   men ne cuðon,
ne ða seglrode   geseon meahton,
eorðbuende   ealle cræfte,
hu afæstnod wæs   feldhusa mæst,
siððan he mid wuldre   geweorðode
þeodenholde.
                   'The warriors looked with wonder,
most joyous of hosts. The day-shield's protection
was flung across the skies; wise God
had covered with a sail the course of the sun,
although all the craft of earth-dwelling men
neither knew the mastropes nor might understand the sail,
how the greatest of tents was established
after he was honored with glory, with faith.'

The baffling imagery in this passage has sent many a scholar in search of a source. Samuel Moore explained it by saying that it is in keeping with the Old English fondness for the sea.[33] Irving suggests that the nautical imagery may have occurred to the poet as a result of St. Jerome's definition in his *Liber de Niminibus Hebraicis* of Etham as *consummatus sive suscipiens navigationem.*[34]

Irving's note comments on the description of the Israelites as sailors and the likening of their flight to a voyage but he is more interested at this point in the problem of the clouds and the etymologies of names in the itinerary. Several critics have noticed the sailor motif, most recently Peter J. Lucas, who associates cloud, tabernacle, and Ark into a thematic unity and defends the presence of the Noah episode.[35] However, when the association of the Red Sea crossing with baptism is recalled, I think that the significance of the nautical motif can be carried one step farther and be seen as the Christian's voluntary commitment of himself to the difficult search through life for his *patria*. This allegorical significance of the seafarer motif is substantiated by the comparison of the Egyptians with land-dwellers. We have seen the same motif at work in *The Seafarer*. The *eorðbuende* do not understand sea-craft; the man who has turned toward earthly glory can neither have insight

33 Samuel Moore, "On the Sources of the Old English Exodus", p. 107.
34 Irving's edition, note on *segle*, p. 74.
35 Peter J. Lucas, "The Cloud in the Interpretation of the Old English

into the Christian exile's commitment to his way of life nor understand his faith in the grace of God which he feels certain awaits
him at the end of his voyage.

The pillars enter the poem at line 94b, after the Israelite host
has stopped at Etham. Their function on this appearance is significant. They have come to measure the campsite at Etham. This
act of measuring suggests the controlling presence of God, who
defines and sets limits. The pillars, therefore, represent the controlling power of God in the life of the Israelite people. The notion
of control anticipates the function of the fiery pillar as a threat to
those who do not obey the commands of Moses. The pillars and
the cloud at Guðmyrce, therefore, represent different aspects of
God's presence among His people, the one controlling, the other
protective.

Lines 103b–106a carry forward all the images discussed above:
the controlling power of God through Moses, God's presence in the
pillars which set the way, the Israelites as seamen, and the exodus
as a sea journey:

> Forð gesawon
> lifes latþeow   lifweg metan;
> swegl siðe weold,   sæmen æfter
> foron flodwege.
>
> 'They saw go before them
> life's leader measuring out the path of life;
> the cloud governed the way; the seamen following,
> went forth on the sea.'

The most troublesome word in the passage is *flodwege*. The direct
reference to the sea seems at first glance so out of place at this
point that there has been an unwillingness to accept the literal
translation. Grein suggested emendation to *foldwege*.[36] Irving and
R. K. Gordon translate "on the road to the sea". Kennedy gives
"through the great waters", Blackburn reads "by (on, along) the
road to the sea", and Thorpe gives the literal "the floodway".[37]

Exodus", *ES*, LI (1970), 297-311.
[36]   Blackburn's edition, p. 8.
[37]   Irving's edition, p. 75; R. K. Gordon, *Anglo-Saxon Poetry*, p. 125;
Kennedy, *The Caedmon Poems*, p. 102; Blackburn's edition, p. 40; Benjamin
Thorpe, *Caedmon's Paraphrase* (London, 1832), p. 184.

Irving notes that the images of the poem bear out the manuscript reading of *flodwege* as a reference to the sea itself, although he gives the more cautious translation. The fact that other aspects of the poem strengthen the argument in favor of allegorical interpretation paradoxically strengthens the possibility that the literal meaning of the manuscript word is precisely the one intended and that the translation of the passage as I have given it is the sense in which the audience would have taken it. As I have said above, the nature of early medieval allegory is such that the concrete details and the allegory cannot be separated. They are warp and woof of the one fabric. Allegorically, the seafarer is the man who has committed his life to doing God's will on earth. He has placed himself completely under the power and protection of God, represented in *Exodus* by the covering cloud in the land of Guðmyrce and later by the pillars of cloud and fire at Etham. This interpretation is anticipated and completed by the contrast (84ff.) with the land-dwellers (*eorðbuende*) who do not understand sea life.

The sea enters the poem again at line 118b:

```
115                        heofoncandel barn.
     Niwe nihtweard      nyde sceolde
     wician ofer weredum,      þy læs him westengryre,
     har hæðbroga,       holmegum wederum
     on ferclamme        ferhð getwæfde.
```

> 'heaven's candle burned.
> The new night-guardian must of need
> remain over the host, lest they suddenly be seized
> by the terror of the desert, the hoary heath monster,
> be deprived of their spirit by the sea winds.'

Although this translation does not settle all the problems of case in the difficult passage, particularly in the word *hæðbroga*, it does create what seems a defensible sense in the lines: it was necessary that the burning pillar (*heofoncandel*) remain in evidence over the host in order to strengthen their spirits, lest they lose faith and allow themselves to be driven away from their purpose by the fears and doubts that often beset the faithful in their carrying out of God's will. The Bible story, Exodus 13:17, records such a fear in the Israelites, a fear which led Moses to take a route which avoided the Philistines, for fear that the threat of fighting might make the people regret their decision to flee and turn back toward Egypt. That the Old English poet chose not to use the fear motif at the beginning of the journey but to save it for its present place in the poem is significant. In the allegorical structure, the situation of the Israelites at Etham is critical: they have received incontrovertible proof of the presence of God in their mission, a proof which, paradoxically, puts them to the sternest temptation. Having received this proof, they can no longer avoid the recognition of the difficult nature of the task ahead; if they proceed and accept the full implication of this divine mission, which will manifest itself in the miracle of the sea passage, their lot will have been cast and any falling away henceforth will be immeasurably more damning. The relationship to the situation of the catechumen, as has been pointed out by Bright, is obvious. We have a clear statement of this relationship in the twelfth-century commentary of Bruno Astensis in his *Exposito in Exodum*, where he writes: *Merito igitur de Sochot, id est de tabernaculis, venitur in Ethan, quia postquam ad Ecclesiam homo veniens baptizatus est, non otiosus sedere, sed per hujus maris pericula cum apostolis navigare debet . . .Venit igitur populus de Ethan in Aharoth, quia jam coepta navigatione, quibusdam virtutum gradibus proficiens, venit ad coronam.*[38] This is the point at which the Israelites have to make a final choice, the point at which the fear of what they are about to undertake on the sea and in the desert becomes most intense. It is at this point that God's presence in the pillars becomes of greatest importance.

The phrase central to the discussion of the nautical imagery is, of course, *holmegum wederum*. Kennedy and R. K. Gordon translate simply "stormy weather", while Thorpe gives "raging storms".[39] Irving reads "By storms of a violence usually only encountered at sea", although (compare his treatment of *foldwege*, above) he suggests that

metaphorically the poet seems once more to be carrying out his

[38]   Cited in Irving's edition, p. 74.
[39]   Kennedy, *The Caedmon Poems*, p. 102; R. K. Gordon, *Anglo-Saxon Poetry*, p. 125; Thorpe, *Caedmon's Paraphrase*, p. 185.

nautical figure which has been so far extended already – these are "sea-storms" which threaten the Israelite "sailors" and their ship (of faith, presumably).[40]

In spite of his apparent recognition of the image, he insists on the more cautious reading. Again, it seems to me that Irving, had he accepted his own implications, could have arrived at a more suitable translation. The imagery is the same as that in *The Seafarer,* where the storms represent the buffeting of the world of fears and doubts, which fears and doubts are the obstacles to fulfilment of the Christian commitment. We have noted similar image patterns in patristic writing. Such an interpretation of the *Exodus* passage seems most reasonable once the allegorical character of the narrative is established. The interpretation serves, in turn, to strengthen the argument for allegorical interpretation of *The Seafarer,* where the context is not so obviously religious.

In the following passage, lines 125ff., the Israelites make their way to the Red Sea and their fourth encampment. At line 133a occurs another reference to the Israelites as seamen, *flotan:*

                 Fyrdwic aras;
130 wyrpton hie werige,   wiste genægdon
     modige meteþegnas,   hyra mægen beton.
     Bræddon æfter beorgum,   siððan byme sang,
     flotan feldhusum.

                'A camp arose;
weary, they relaxed; meat-thanes approached
the noble ones with food, restored their strength.
Then they spread out among the hills after the trumpet sang,
the sailors in their tents.'

Here again we have the sailor image together with that of the tents, and we recall Gollancz's early and Lucas' more recent comment on the equating of tents and tabernacles. The unusually compressed syntax which characterizes the poem is particularly significant here. The phrase *flotan feldhusum,* from which the prepositions and modifiers are omitted, produces an unusually close juxtaposition of the sailors and their tents; it is as if the phrase meant some-

40 Irving's edition, p. 76.

thing like 'tented sailors' or 'tabernacled sailors'. Such verbal econ-
omy and compression of ideas is not widely characteristic of Old
English poetry, and the frequency with which it occurs in *Exodus*
makes it worthy of comment, particularly in a figurative passage
such as this one. The association of the Israelites with the tabernacles emphasizes the fact of God's protecting presence as the
people approach their miraculous deliverance. In the allegorical
significance of baptism, the water symbolism is meaningful on both
the literal and symbolic levels.

Further evidence in favor of an allegorical interpretation of the
passage lies in another possible pun, which, to my knowledge, has
not been noted before. The pun is in the word *beorgum*. The primary meaning of the word is 'a hill, mountain', but the word is
related to the German *burg* and its various forms. Bosworth-Toller
gives a secondary meaning of 'a protection, refuge', which meaning
fits perfectly the allegorical sense of the passage. Not only are the
Israelites described as spreading about upon the hills (itself an
image of striking beauty), they are also described as resting in the
knowledge of God's protecting presence. The images both of hill
and of a fortified place strengthen the notions of endurance and
security. But the introduction of this sense of security into the poem
at this point makes for a significant bit of irony, for it is immediately after this passage that the Israelites hear rumors of the pursuit
of the Egyptians and are thrown into fear. Having received the
assurance of God's presence in their journey, the Israelites are now
warned against complacency by the knowledge that the forces of
evil are never at rest. It is an admirably realistic psychological
touch.

The next image that fits the pattern occurs at line 179b:

>   Freond onsegon
> laðum eagan   landmanna cyme.

> 'The host watched
> with hostile eyes the approach of the land men.'

As the Israelites prepare for battle, they watch the approach of the
Egyptian army. The Egyptians are described as 'land men'.
Literally, the word *landmanna* is a reference to the direction from

which the army is approaching. However, we have had before, in the passage concerning the protecting cloud covering, the deliberate contrast between the Israelite 'sailors' and the 'earthdwellers'. The earlier passage does not specifically name the earthdwellers but there can be little doubt that the figure refers to those who do not place their faith in God, the Egyptian host and its leader, Pharaoh, who represent the world and the devil. The Israelites are significantly at this point on the shores of the Red Sea, on the very brink of their commitment.

The next reference to the Israelites as seamen occurs at line 223a.

```
220                    Snelle gemundon
        weardas wigleoð,     werod wæs gefysed,
        brudon ofer burgum,     (byman gehyrdon),
        flotan feldhusum,     fyrd wæs on ofste.
```

'The guardians quickly heeded the summons of the / trumpet; the host, the sailors in their tents, / spread abroad over the hills, was readied when / the trumpet was heard; the army stirred itself / hastily.'

We notice immediately that line 223a is an exact repetition of 133a, in fact, that 222–223a are close verbal parallels with 132–133a:

```
132 Bræddon æfter beorgum,     siððan byme sang,
       flotan feldhusum.

222 brudon ofer burgum,     (byman gehyrdon),
       flotan feldhusum.
```

The repetition of the *beorgum-burgum* forms, followed in both passages by the insistence on the Israelites as seamen, makes for interesting speculation. Even granting the formal character of Old English poetic language (of all poetic language, for that matter), it seems hardly likely that such a conspicuous repetition could have been fortuitous. It seems much more likely that the poet was carrying out his allegorical theme of Christian salvation and the security of God's presence in the lives of men.

The allegorical interpretation of the passage is substantiated by two other figures, although neither is part of the nautical imagery:

the appearance of the word *eðelrihtes* at line 211b and the dawn image at 216a. Line 211 states that in their fear of the oncoming Egyptians the Israelites had lost their faith that they would ever attain their *eðelrihtes*, their 'rights of homeland'. This translation, rather than Kennedy's 'inheritance' seems justified, since the word translates the Latin *patriam jus*.[41] On the literal or cortex level, the word denotes the fear of the Israelites that they will never see their promised homeland, but as a sign the word suggests the situation of the earthly exile in search of the City of God. The fear on this level is tantamount to a loss of faith, to despair in the face of mounting hardship. I have already discussed the double meaning of *eðel* as both earthly and heavenly abodes in my interpretation of *The Seafarer*.

The dawn image, although it is a more literal sight image than is the reference to the *eðelrihtes*, has significant overtones. Dawn has a traditional value as a figure representing the coming of knowledge or hope. The same image figures in the opening lines of *The Wanderer*, where it suggests the first hint of the wanderer's awareness of his situation. In the *Exodus* passage, Moses, as dawn breaks, is calling together the fearful Israelites to encourage their faith and to exhort them to valor in the coming fight. The fact that their fear is strongest during the nighttime hours and that they receive the message exhorting them to bravery with the coming of light seems definitely to imply some connection between the message and the light.

A new nautical image enters the poem at line 333a, one which has never been satisfactorily interpreted.

> Æfter þære fyrde   flota modgade,
> Rubenes sunu.   Randas bæron
> sæwicingas   ofer sealtne mersc.

> 'After that army of proud seamen,
> Reuben's sons. They bore their shields,
> the sea vikings, over the salt marsh.'

Scholars have consistently associated the *flota modgade* with the

---

[41]   Bosworth-Toller; Irving, in the glossary to his edition, gives "RIGHTS to a country".

sons of Reuben and have thereby created a major difficulty. No one has been able to explain why the tribe of Reuben should be signalled out for praise, particularly since there is apparently nothing in Jewish tradition to substantiate either such praise or such an interpretation of the passage.

The lines occur just before the passage which describes the fighting in the van of the Israelite retreat toward the sea and they name the fourth tribe, that of Judah, as leading the way *on uncuð gelad* (compare line 58b). Since the form *flota* can be more easily construed as a genitive plural than anything else, and since *modgade* is obviously adjectival, the phrase can easily be read as referring to the tribe of Judah. In such an interpretation, the phrase *flota modgade* loses some of its effect and thereby implies less emphasis on the sons of Reuben than in the usual translation. The word *sæwicingas*, usually taken as a reference exclusively to the sons of Reuben, can then be read as the poet's expansion of the notion of bravery to cover all of God's people, not just one tribe. Such a brave fight as Judah is described as having put up in the lines immediately preceding the passage under discussion supplies ample reason for the praise given by the poet in his designating the tribe *flota modgade*. And the use of the words *flota* and *sæwicingas* to designate the sons of Judah and Reuben carries forward the allegorical contrast between the sea-man and the land dweller.

One further point should be made. The church militant is to be seen in the allegory at this point. Since the passage through water is to be related to the sacrament of baptism, it is necessary that we be aware of the meaning of the word 'sacrament'. During the early Middle Ages, the word still carried the meaning of an oath taken by Roman soldiers, so that the notion of commitment to battle is strong. Cross and Tucker emphasize the relevance of this meaning in the word by pointing out that the fighting faced by Judah immediately upon acceptance of the miraculous act signifies the Christian view that the catechumen comes to baptism as a soldier to the colors.[42] Such interpretation of the fighting against the

---

[42] Cross and Tucker, "Allegorical Tradition and the Old English Exodus", p. 125.

Egyptians gives further reason for the poet's desire to attribute
such bravery to all Israelites rather than to one tribe only. Further,
the fighting that the Israelites face at the very beginning of their
journey serves as warning that their exile will be one of struggle
and hardship to the end.

The Noah and Abraham stories enter the poem at line 362.
The nautical images that occur therein will be discussed in the section of the chapter devoted to these stories.

The next thematic motif to be discussed is that of the treasure
of the Israelites, which enters the poem in its closing lines. These
final lines have constituted one of the most baffling cruces of the
poem, particularly in the images of the *Afrisc Neowle* at line 580b
and of the *ealde madmas* at line 586b. The *Afrisc Neowle* crux is
not involved in the allegorical interpretation, but the case of the
ealde madmas 'ancient treasure' is another story, particularly since
it is an addition of the poet to the biblical source. We are told at
Exodus 12:35 that the Israelites, prior to their departure, asked
vessels of gold and silver and much raiment of the Egyptians,
which the Egyptians lent to them, but there is no mention in the
Bible narrative of the treasure which the Israelites came into possession of after the crossing.[43] Jewish legend states that the
treasure was taken by the Israelites from the sea following the destruction of the Egyptian host, and it is to this legend, as recorded in
a no longer extent Latin version, that the poet of *Exodus* must have
gone for his source.[44] The story had wide circulation during the
early Middle Ages and was almost certainly the source of the
exegetical tradition that the treasure represented God's truth
whereas the idols which had fallen on the departure of the Israelites represented the false beliefs of the pagans.[45] The poet's addition of the story to the poem indicates beyond a reasonable doubt
that he felt certain of his audience's recognition of the allegorical
significance. Finally, the story fits the symbolic treatment of the
baptism motif perfectly. Since baptism is the first of the church's

[43] For a discussion of the treasure given the Israelites on their departure
from Egypt, see Josephus, *Works*, 2nd ed., trans. William Whiston, introduction by the Rev. H. Stebbing (Philadelphia, n.d.), p. 83 n.
[44] Louis Ginsberg, *Legends of the Bible* (Philadelphia, 1956), pp. 344, 358.
[45] Bernard Huppé, *Doctrine and Poetry*, p. 4; Irving's edition, p. 96.

sacraments, it is the catechumen's introduction to the treasure of God's truth as revealed in the church's teaching.

The final structural motif of the poem to be dealt with is the place of the Noah and Abraham stories, which are told beginning at line 362. The references in the Noah story to Noah as a sea-prince and to the ship and to sailing are natural. They are so natural, in fact, that their function as a part of the imagery which unites the Noah story with the rest of the poem is easy to overlook. The same may be said of the reference to Abraham as an exile. Much early scholarship considered the stories interpolations, and some scholars even gave this section of the poem separate names, such as "Noah und anderer Patriarchen".[46] Later scholars omitted the passage.[47] However, some scholars have defended the passage's integrity, particularly Gollancz, Blackburn, Krapp, Irving, and Greenfield.[48] Gollancz, Krapp, and Irving have suggested more strongly that the stories have a definite part in the development of the theme of the poem. Their argument, generally stated, is that the stories of Noah and Abraham are stories of flood and of God's covenant with His chosen people, both of which themes have an important place in the poem's development. A more detailed defense of the centrality of the stories is possible if we take a careful look at the way in which the thematic structures which have been discussed in this chapter are woven throughout lines 362–446, particularly the four themes of the covenant, exile, nautical imagery, and treasure.

The nautical imagery appears at lines 362, *Niwe flodas Noe oferlað*; 364, *þone deopestan drencefloda*; 367, *ofer lagustreamas*; 374, *snottor sæleoda*; 375, *on bearm scipes*. These five images, occurring in the short space of 18 lines, structure sharply the story of Noah, the wise sea leader, sailing over the perilous sea-ways in his great ship, bearing seeds of every living kind, *maðmhorda mæst* 'the richest of treasure-hoards' (368a). The ship in exeget-

---

[46] Alois Brandl, *Grundriss der germanischen Philologie*, ed. H. Paul, 2nd ed. (Strassburg, 1908), II, 1029. Cited in Irving's edition, p. 8.

[47] W. J. Sedgefield, *An Anglo-Saxon Book of Verse and Prose*, p. 95.

[48] Gollancz, *The Caedmon Manuscript*, pp. lxxiiff; Blackburn's edition, pp. 53ff; Krapp, *The Junius Manuscript*, p. xxviii; Irving's edition, pp. 8-9; Greenfield, *A Critical History of Old English Literature*, pp. 154ff.

ical allegory is almost always the church, in other words, the law, the covenant, as handed down from Abraham through Moses. All four of these thematic motifs are telescoped into the short passage, and all four function to weave the episode into the structure of the poem. The seas are the unpredictable hardships of a life devoted to the doing of God's will. The exile motif is also sharply drawn. Noah was not only exiled on the face of the deep during the five months of his voyage but he was also ostracized by his neighbors and stood their scorn during the days preceding the flood when he stood unwavering in his faith. The covenant motif enters the episode at two places: at line 366, where Noah is spoken of as cherishing the *halige treowa* 'holy covenant', and at 386, where Noah is described as sailing across the ocean streams bearing *maðmhorda mæst*. The treasure-hoard is, of course, the cargo of life, but this cargo and the wisdom Noah shows and the care he exercises in his protection of it symbolize Noah's carrying out of the covenant, which is also a great treasure for mankind, as has been established in the opening lines of the poem.

There is one other problem, connected in one sense with the entire passage, in another sense more directly with the Noah story. The problem involves the translation of the opening two words of line 362, *Niwe flodas*. Blackburn found the transition from the preceding material abrupt. Irving has also said that the transition is "at best rather abrupt and surprising".[49] Literally translated, the phrase *Niwe flodas* means 'new floods', which is at best vague. Thorpe emended to *Niþe flodas* 'dire floods', creating a different but smoother thought, if the only alternative is the literal reading of *niwe*.[50] However, *niwe* has connotations which, when applied, seem to solve the problem. The word suggests 'strange' or 'as yet unknown' and is meant to tell the audience that they are going to hear a story of a different kind of flood. The intensity of meaning in *drencefloda* (see Irving's note on emendation here) at line 364b substantiates the broadened meaning.

Irving has made a penetrating comment on the passage, which bears directly upon the problem at hand. He suggests that the

[49]   Blackburn's edition, p. 53; Irving's edition, p. 8.
[50]   Thorpe, *Caedmon's Paraphrase*, p. 200 n.

comparison of the floods is not the point which the poet was trying
to make but that it is, rather, a comparison of the voyage of Noah
and the allegorical 'voyage' of the Israelites 'over' the Red Sea.[51]
Seeing the Israelite crossing as a voyage relates the Noah story to
the symbolic theme of the poem in two ways. First, it ties the Noah
episode to the covenant theme, since the pillars, which function as
both guide and warning, and the cloud-cover at Guðmyrce, which
functions as protection, symbolize God's keeping of His covenant
with His people. Second, it relates the Noah story to the allegory
of the journey of life as a sea voyage. Both the biblical story and
the poem bear the interpretation.

The transition from the Noah story to that of Abraham is not
only syntactically smooth, it emphasizes the thematic development.
The motifs developed in the episode are those of exile and covenant, and they are introduced within the first twelve lines of the
story. Both the themes are utilized in the poem and are so close to
the Bible story that repetition of them seems unnecessary. It is
necessary only to point out that the themes carry through a
thematic development which is in the entire poem.

There is another aspect of the Abraham story which seems
significant. Abraham's willingness to sacrifice his son, particularly
since Abraham is the father image in the poem, would carry
the implication of God's willingness to sacrifice His Son for
the salvation of mankind. The idea of sacrifice is of central importance to the meaning of the covenant. The audience would have
been reminded of the great sacrifice which God had made for them,
the fullest meaning of which they must become aware as a part of
the sacrament of baptism. The placing of this story of sacrifice immediately after the entrance of the Israelites into the sea puts the
thematic emphasis on the full meaning of the sacramental passage
through the waters – the Christian's acceptance of his part in the
death of Christ and his acceptance of the life of exile. The fact that
the destruction of the Egyptian host by these same waters follows
immediately upon the Abraham story completes the development
of the motif of the miraculous and protecting power of the church's
sacraments. The holy water in this destructive act cleanses from

[51] Irving's edition, p. 89.

the Christian all the sins that have pursued him and threatened his faith. This cleansing from evil is the cause of the Israelites' rejoicing on the opposite shore and of the Canticle of Moses, the message of which made clear to the Israelites the power and truth of God's word. It is significant also that only after this moral has been made plain is the 'ancient treasure' divided among the standards. The 'ancient treasure', having come from the sea, is, of course, the Christian's assurance of the truth of God's word. It is what he has gained from his experience with sin, and it is his cleansing through the sacrament of baptism.

Since all these major themes can be seen developed in the Noah and Abraham episodes, it seems reasonable to assume that the stories are not at all interpolations but are integral to the development of the theme of the poem. The theme of *Exodus* would seem to be that of the Christian's struggle against the sins of the world, his battle to keep faith in the face of almost overwhelming hardships, and the part which the sacraments of the church, particularly baptism, play in the strengthening of the Christian in his determination to keep faith and fulfil the covenant which God instituted through the sacrifice of His Son for man.

VI

CYNEWULF

Since Benjamin Thorpe brought out his edition of *The Exeter Book* in 1842, most of the scholarship on the material contained in the first 1664 lines of that Old English codex has been centered around two problems: one, the unity and authorship of the three sections into which the manuscript material is divided, and, two, the identity of Cynewulf, whose name appears in runes in the closing lines of the second section. There is still great lack of agreement as to the unity and authorship of the lines, and the identity of the man Cynewulf has never been established nor does it appear at this time likely to be.[1] I shall not deal here with the iden-

---

[1] See, for instance, Moritz Trautmann, "Der sogenannte Crist", *Anglia*, XVIII (1896), 382-388; F. A. Blackburn, "Is the 'Christ' of Cynewulf a Single Poem?", *Anglia*, XIX (1897), 88-98; M. Bentinck Smith, "Old English Christian Poetry", *CHEL* (New York, 1907); Albert S. Cook (ed.), *The Christ of Cynewulf* (Boston, 1909); G. H. Gerould, "Studies in the Christ", *Engl. Stud.*, XLI (1910), 1-19; Samuel Moore, "The Old English Christ: Is It a Unit?", *JEGP*, XIV (1915), 550-567; Edward Burgert, *The Dependence of Part I of Cynewulf's Christ on the Antiphonary* (Washington, D.C., 1921); E. E. Wardale, *Chapters on Old English Literature* (London, 1935), pp. 150ff; Br. Augustine Philip, "The Exeter Scribe and the Unity of the Christ", *PMLA*, LV (1940), 903-909; Charles W. Kennedy, *The Earliest English Poetry* (New York, 1943), pp. 198ff, esp. 220-221; Karl Mildenberger, "Unity of Cynewulf's Christ in the Light of Iconography", *Spec.*, XXIII (1948), 426-432; Claes Schaar, *Critical Studies in the Cynewulf Group* (Lund, 1949); Kenneth Sisam, "Cynewulf and His Poetry", *Studies in the History of Old English Literature* (Oxford, 1953); J. J. Campbell, *The Advent Lyrics of the Exeter Book* (Princeton, 1959); Stanley B. Greenfield, *A Critical History of Old English Literature* (New York, 1965), p. 124; C. L. Wrenn, *A Study of Old English Literature* (London, 1967), pp. 123ff, esp. 126; Robert B. Burlin, *The Old English Advent: A Typological Commentary* (New Haven, 1968), among others.

tity of Cynewulf; however, I will suggest in my conclusion that, in spite of the number of arguments to the contrary, I feel that there is strong evidence for the unity of the 1664 lines, which conclusion implies an acceptance of a likelihood of singleness of authorship.

The poem occupies folios 8a–32a of *The Exeter Book* and begins, apparently, in mid-sentence. The manuscript indicates breaks at lines 439 and 866. The breaks are generally accepted as indicating divisions of the material. Cook and Moore stand all but alone in their defense of the unity of the three divisions. One of Cook's most telling arguments is that it is much easier to argue for disunity than for unity. He set up the hypothetical situation of the discovery of the various groups of poems which comprise Tennyson's *Maud* and pointed out the obvious difficulty of attempting to ascertain unity of authorship of such a body of work.[2]

As to the identity of the poet, four suggestions have been made: Cenwulf (Cynwulf) of Mercia, a contemporary of Aldhelm, who died in 709; Cynewulf, bishop of Lindisfarne, who died in 782; Cynulf, a clergyman who attended the synod of Cloveshoe in 803; and Cenwulf, abbot of Peters borough, who died in 1014.

Greenfield, in 1953, took what appears to be a significant step in the right direction to solving the questions of theme and unity. He attempted to find the meaning of the poem in its historical theological relationships.[3] In this attempt he follows the lead of scholars such as Robertson, Huppé, Lumiansky, and Smithers, in their work on the elegies, and of Irving, Cross, and Tucker on the Caedmonian *Exodus*. Greenfield works carefully through Part I of *Christ*, pointing out references therein to the theme of spiritual exile, a theme which has been shown in this study to be central not only to exegetical and patristic tradition before and during the time when the Old English poems were being composed, but also to the Old English poems themselves. Greenfield's work has pointed out perhaps the most important aspect of the religious nature of the poetry, an aspect which I emphasized in the introductory chapter to the elegies: the artistic development of a definite thematic struc-

---

[2]   See Cook's edition, pp. lxxii-lxxiii.
[3]   Greenfield, "The Theme of Spiritual Exile in Christ I", *PQ*, XXXII (1953), 321-328.

ture. Earlier scholars were loath to consider the poems seriously as artistic accomplishments, seeing unity in them, if unity they saw at all, only in sources and genres. The approach to the poems represented in the work of Greenfield not only gives the poets their long-overdue recognition as artists but also goes directly to the heart of the poems.

The approach I shall take to the poem *Christ* is largely that suggested by Greenfield; however, I shall carry his suggestions farther than he did. I shall attempt to show that the theme of spiritual exile exists not only in Part I of the poem but that it also forms the central thematic structure for all three parts and in so doing constitutes a strong argument in favor of the unity of the whole. I shall point also to other structural elements such as (1) Christ as the guardian or 'lock', noted by Greenfield, (2) nautical imagery as associated with the exile theme, including the contrast between seafarers and land-dwellers, which structure appeared in the elegies and in *Exodus*, and (3) word play, particularly on the word *sunu*, also noted by Greenfield. The presence of these carefully worked out structures in the entire body of the material seems to me strong evidence for its artistic integrity and weighs heavily on the side of those who argue in favor of single authorship.

My only argument with Greenfield is that he did not carry his study far enough to see its relevance to the entire poem.

There are in Part I a number of references to the figure of the exile which Greenfield did not point out. I shall first cite these images and then discuss such related imagic structures as the 'lock' figure, nautical imagery, and word play. The first of such figures appears in a passage beginning at line 22:

> Huru we for þearfe   þas word sprecað,
> ond m[. . .]giað   þone þe mon gescop
> þæt he ne [.]ete[. . .]ceose weorðan
> 25 cearfulra þing,   þe we in carcerne
> sittað sorgende,   sunnan wenað,
> hwonne us liffrea   leoht ontyne.

> 'Indeed, we in need speak these words
> and beseech Him who made man
> that He not choose to speak in hate

> to us wretched things, we who sit sorrowing
> in the prison house, who await the sun,
> whence the Lord of life will release to us the light.'

The exile figure is in the phrase *in carcerne* 'in the prison house'. Throughout the early Middle Ages we find reference to the world in which man is exiled as a prison or as some other kind of captivity.[4] The use of the phrase *cearfulra þing* at 25a presents one further interesting possibility. The fact that those waiting in prison are referred to as 'things' suggests that without Christ's saving power they are inanimate, that is, that without the Son they have no life.

Another point to be considered is that most translators read *hwonne*, 27a, as 'until'.[5] The word, however, can also mean 'whence', which reading seems to give the lines much greater significance as part of the exile pattern by emphasizing the source of the exiles' salvation. Most important of all, this emphasis calls attention to a pun on the word *sunnan*, 26b, a pun which is repeated frequently in Part I and also occurs in Parts II and III. Although I shall develop the pun motif separately, the translation of the lines here makes necessary my dealing with this particular pun at this time. That the exiles are in the prison house of the world, locked in the darkness of sin, yearning for the 'sun', cannot fail to mean that they yearn for the Son, the Savior, who, at His Second Advent at the Last Judgment, will free the faithful exiles from death. The Catholic belief that the bodies of the dead will rise at the Last Judgment and that the faithful will receive their reward of eternal paradise is, of course, central to the idea of freeing from death. The image of the hosts of the dead rising at Judgment is an important part of the development of the theme in Part III. The pun at this

---

[4]   See, for instance, Gregory's likening of life to a dungeon in the *Dialogues*, p. 190. See also *The Pulpit Commentary*, I, 480-481, and *The Expositor's Bible*, I, 378, where the imprisonment of Joseph's brothers is construed as God's trial of man's faith. See also St. John Chrysostum, *Homilies on the Acts of the Apostles and the Epistle to the Romans*, in *Nicene and Post-Nicene Fathers*, XI, 430, where mortal life is construed as captivity to the law of sin.

[5]   See, for instance, Gollancz, *The Exeter Book*, Pt. I, p. 5, and R. K. Gordon, *Anglo-Saxon Poetry*, p. 148.

point is too central to the religious theme to have been anything but deliberate.

The figure reappears at line 50:

> Eala sibbe gesihð,   sancta Hierusalem,
> cynestola cyst,   Cristes burglond.

> 'O vision of peace, holy Jerusalem,
> most magnificent of royal thrones, city of Christ.'

The reference here to Jerusalem suggests the City of God as contrasted with the city of the earth, the distinction made by St. Augustine. The city of the earth is symbolic of man's mortal life, in which he must, as an exile from paradise, seek through faith his return to the City of God. The apostrophe to the holy city is based on the Advent antiphon *O Hierusalem* and follows immediately a passage based on the antiphon *O Clavis David*. The *O Clavis David* passage contains a crux at line 19a, *se þe locan healeð*, which Greenfield interprets figuratively as a reference to Christ. In his interpretation, Christ, as a member of the line of David, becomes the key who controls the locks on the gates to paradise. The figure of the lock, or more literally, the guardian of the lock, occurs, as I have indicated, throughout the poem. Attention should be called here to the multiple levels of irony in the implication that Christ controls not only the key, or lock, which will open the gates to paradise and the key, or lock, which will open the gates to free the exiles from their earthly prison, but also that He controls the key, or lock, which will free the good pagans from Limbo in the harrowing of hell, and finally, the key, or lock, which will close the gates of hell forever upon the damned. Greenfield's explanation of the images makes clear the poet's development of his theme. The passage containing the lock image, being based on the antiphon *O Clavis David*, is logically followed by a passage based on the *O Hierusalem*. Since Jerusalem suggests, on the anagogical level, the City of God, the heavenly home which the Christian exiles seek, the sequence of passages implies that it is this holy city to which Christ holds the key and to which He has the power to admit the exiles, who are described in lines 31–32 as waiting in abject plight, bereft of home. The *O Hierusalem* itself supplied the poet the reference to the allegory of earthly exile:

> O Hierusalem, civitas Dei summi: leva in circuitu oculos tuos, et vide Dominum tuum, quia jam veniet solvere te a vinculis.

'O, Jerusalem, city of the great God, lift up thine eyes round about, and see thy Lord, for he is coming to loose thee from thy chains.'[6]

The loosing from the chains of bondage also suggests the action of Christ as the key.

Closely following at lines 66ff. is another example of the figure:

	Nu is þæt bearn cymen,
awæcned to wyrpe	weorcum Ebrea,
bringeð blisse þe,	benda onlyseð
niþum genedde.	Nearoþearfe conn,
70 hu se earm sceal	are gebidan.

'Now the child is come,
born to complete the labors of the Hebrews;
He brings you bliss, He loosens bonds
forged in malice. He understands pressing need,
how the wretched must await mercy.'

Here again are the wretched exiles, awaiting in the prison house the mercy of God, suffering the pains of sin. Line 68b makes reference to the fact that Christ will now loosen the bonds, a standard figure for the effect of God's mercy upon the exile, as we have seen frequently in the elegies. Note also the verbal correspondence between line 70b and line 1b of *The Wanderer*.

A similar figure occurs in lines 146b–148a:

	Nu hie softe þæs
bidon in bendum	hwonne bearn godes
cwome to cearigum.	

'The oppressed have awaited patiently
in their bonds the time when the Child of God
would come.'

The oppressed endure their bonds patiently, awaiting the freeing power of Christ. In a figurative situation of this kind time operates

6 Cook's edition, pp. 72, 81.

on multiple levels. We have the oppressed Israelites fulfilling their covenant with God; typologically, we have the prefiguring of the condition of the faithful just prior to the Nativity; and, finally, we have the eschatological anticipation of the Second Advent and the Last Judgment. In the Christian context, Christ is the key to the misery of the exile. Once this figure of Christ as the key or guardian of the lock is established, any mention of bonds or of freeing from bonds recalls it. It becomes part of the chain of associated notions which accumulate as the theme develops.

The first of the nautical images to be associated with exile appears in lines 219–23.

> Nis ænig nu   eorl under lyfte,
> secg searoþoncol,   to þæs swiðe gleaw
> þe þæt asecgan mæge   sundbuendum,
> areccan mid ryhte,   hu þe rodera weard
> æt frymðe genom   him to freobearne.

> 'There is now no man beneath the heavens,
> no man cunning or sufficiently wise,
> who can say to the ocean-dwellers,
> and tell it right, how the guardian of the skies
> at the beginning took Himself a lordly Son.'

Recent translators read *sundbuendum* figuratively, and with validity, as 'mortals' or 'people'; however, for the purposes of my thesis I return to Gollancz's literal 'ocean-dwellers', which reading seems more exactly to the point the poet was trying to make.[7] The figure is completely unmotivated here and enters the poem with striking suddenness. The lack of motivation and the resulting effect of suddenness may well indicate that the poet felt no need either to prepare for the use of the figure or to explain it in any way, that he could count on his audience to be aware of its significance. Perhaps even more important is the indication of the poet's artistic ability in his use of such deliberate suddenness for effect. The meaning of the word *sundbuendum* is obviously the same as the meaning utilized by the *Exodus* poet in his reference to the Israelites as seamen.

7 Campbell, p. 62; Burlin, p. 128; Gollancz, *The Exeter Book*, p. 16.

Another suggestion of the condition of exile occurs at the very end of the passage based on the *O Rex Pacifice*:

270   ... þæt we, tires wone,
   a butan ende   sculon ermþu dreogan,
   butan þu usic þon ofostlicor,   ece dryhten,
   æt þam leodsceaþan,   lifgende god,
   helm alwihta,   hreddan wille.

                 '... that we, deprived of glory,
   must endure misery without end
   unless You, eternal Lord,
   living God, guardian of all living things,
   save us in all haste.'

The figure closes a passage of 26 lines built around the image of Christ approaching through formerly locked golden gates to free the world from evil:

   Þu þisne middangeard   milde geblissa
250 þurh ðinne hercyme,   hælende Crist,
   ond þa gyldnan geatu,   þe in geardagum
   ful longe ær   bilocen stodan.

The image of the weary exiles awaiting Christ is present in the antiphon on which the entire passage is based:

   O Rex pacifice, tu ante saecula nate: per auream egredere
                                    portam,
   redemptos tuos visita, et eos illuc revoca unde ruerunt per
                                    culpam.

'O King of peace, that wast born before all ages: come by the golden gate, visit them whom thou hast redeemed, and lead them back to the place whence they fell by sin.'[8]

The antiphon implies the Second Advent and in so doing implies the continuation of man in his exile after the scattering at the Ascension. The antiphon recalls man's attention to the Crucifixion and to the fact that it is through Christ's death on the Cross that salvation has become a possibility. This contention is strengthened by the fact that the Crucifixion image occurs in lines 256ff., just preceding the passage under discussion and that line 261b begins a prayer for the salvation of mankind who have existed in exile since

[8]   Cook's edition, pp. 72, 100.

that sinful act. The sinful act of the Crucifixion and the subsequent
scattering of mankind at the Ascension recall also the sin in the
Garden and the expulsion. The two events have parallel significance
in early medieval Christian allegory.

The only reference to city-dwellers in the poem occurs in lines
337–47:

> Huru þæs biddað   burgsittende
> þæt ðu þa frofre   folcum cyðe,
> þinre sylfre sunu.   Siþþan we motan
> 340 anmodlice   ealle hyhtan,
> nu we on þæt bearn foran   breostum stariað.
> Geþinga us nu   þristum wordum
> þæt he us ne læte   leng owihte
> in þisse deaðdene   gedwolan hyran,
> ac þæt he usic geferge   in fæder rice,
> þær we sorglease   siþþan motan
> wunigan in wuldre   mid weoroda god.

> 'Especially do the city-dwellers pray
> that You proclaim, by Your own Son,
> comfort to men, so that we may
> all with one accord rejoice
> when we see the Child on your breast.
> Pray for us now most earnestly
> that He will never leave us
> to live enslaved in this plain of death,
> but that He will lead us to the Father's kingdom,
> where we may live in joy forever,
> in glory with the God of Hosts.'

The use of the word *burgsittende* in this context suggests strongly
that it is being used in the sense of 'land-dweller'. We have seen
in the elegies and in *Exodus* land-dwellers contrasted with seamen
or seafarers. So used, it suggests those who have not committed
their lives to the Christian ideal of the hard mortal lot but rather
have put their dependence on the false felicity of earthly comfort
and pleasure. But the image is used here in an unusual sense. The
lines are part of another long passage which turns on the architectural imagery of walls, gates, and locks. The passage is based on
the final of the added or monastic "O's", the *O mundi Domina*,
which makes direct reference to the passage in Isaiah in which the

angel interprets Isaiah's prophetic dream of the wondrous gate
eternally locked, through which Christ will come to earth:

> "Ic þe mæg secgan   þæt soð gewearð
> þæt ðas gyldnan gatu   giet sume siþe
> god sylf wile   gæstes mægne
> 320 gefælsian,   fæder ælmihtig,
> ond þurh þa fæstan locu   foldan neosan,
> ond hio þonne æfter him   ece stondað
> simle singales   swa beclysed
> þæt nænig oþer,   nymðe nergend god,
> hy æfre ma   eft onluceð."

The references to unlocking doors or gates come to a point in the
poet's apostrophe to Mary, *þu eart þæt wealldor,* line 328a, and
the statement that Christ will come to earth through Mary. A
second miraculous aspect of the birth is implied in the suggestion
that Christ is endowed with a wondrous key with which He will
relock the walldoor after Him. It is immediately after this passage
that we have the reference to the exiles as city-dwellers. The
unusual sense in which the image is used here results in part from
the fact that it is part of the poet's apostrophe to the Virgin. The
poet describes himself as one of those who have turned away from
God. The figure is a deliberate exaggeration; it is the poet's way
of humbling himself in prayer before the Virgin. Used thus, it
carries forward even more strongly the thematic structure of
references to the Christian exile who seeks his way to salvation.
The images of the plain of death (the world) and of the Father's
kingdom (the City of God) are part of the familiar pattern.

The exile image is present in line 382a:

> Eala seo wlitige,   weorðmynda full,
> heah ond halig,   heofoncund þrynes,
> 380 brade geblissad   geond brytenwongas
> þa mid ryhte sculon   reorderende,
> earme eorðware   ealle mægene
> hergan healice,   nu us hælend god
> wærfæst onwrah   þæt we hine witan moton.

> 'Lo, the beautiful, the glorious,
> high and holy heavenly Trinity,
> widely blessed throughout the plains of earth,

You whom those gifted with speech,
wretched earth-dwellers, should highly praise
with all their might, since the Savior has faithfully
revealed God to us, that we might know Him.'

The *earme eorðware* are, of course, the exiles. It will be noted that
the poet does not often use the word *wracu* or *wræc* to express
the wretched condition of the exile. Neither has he availed himself
of the opportunity of making the same kind of word-play which
we have seen used so often in the poets of *The Wanderer, The Seafarer,* and *Exodus.* The poet's figurative use of words in *Christ* has
been of a more directly allegorical or typological nature. He has,
however, used the pun on *sunu,* and it may be that he used fewer
such puns precisely in order to call attention to the central significance of the play on *sunu.* The first occurrence of this pun at line
26b has already been discussed. Other occurrences are as follows.

          Eala earendel,   engla beorhtast
    105 ofer middangeard   monnum sended,
          ond soðfæsta   sunnan leoma,
          torht ofer tunglas,   þu tida gehwane
          of sylfum þe   symle inlihtes!

          'O brightest Ray of the angels,
          faithful beam of the sun,
          sent to men throughout the world,
          clear beyond all the stars, You Yourself
          will illumine forever.'

It is significant of the artistry of the poet that this pun occurs in
the opening lines of the *O Oriens* passage and follows immediately
the passage based on the antiphon *O Virgo Virginum.* The Son,
the light, issues from the Blessed Virgin. The *O Oriens* antiphon
suggests the pun made by the poet:

          O Oriens, splendor lucis aeternae, et sol justitiae: veni,
          et illumina sedentes in tenebris et umbra mortis.

'O Rising Brightness of the Everlasting Light and Sun of Righteous-
ness: come thou and enlighten those who sit in darkness and the
shadow of death.'[9]

⁹ Cook's edition, pp. 71, 88.

Not only does the antiphon suggest the pun, but it also makes use of the figure of the exiles and the usual images of darkness, suggesting the prison house of the world.

The lines following immediately afterward give another play on *sunu*:

```
        Swa þu, god of gode      gearo acenned,
   110 sunu soðan fæder,         swegles in wuldre
        butan anginne     æfre wære,
        swa þec nu for þearfum        þin agen geweorc
        bideð þurh byldo,        þæt þu þa beorhtan us
        sunnan onsende,        ond þe sylf cyme
        þæt ðu inleohte        þa þe longe ær,
        þrosme beþeahte        ond in þeostrum her,
        sæton sinneahtes;        synnum bifealdne
        deorc deaþes sceadu        dreogan sceoldan.
```

'As you, God of God, begotten perfect,
Son of the true Father, Light of Light,
have existed forever without beginning,
so now your own handiwork in its distress
beseeches You boldly to send us
the bright sun, and to come Yourself
so that You may bring light to those who long
have sat here covered with gloom and darkness,
enfolded in the sin of eternal night,
who have endured the dark shadows of death.'

The lines obviously continue the petition of the *O Oriens* to the Son for His saving grace. The word-play on *sunu* structures the entire passage, and, again, we have the image of the darkness of the prison house.

In the Passus occur the following lines:

```
                          . . . þæt me Gabrihel,
        heofones heagengel,      hælo gebodade.
        Sægde soðlice      þæt me swegles gæst
        leoman onlyhte,      sceolde ic lifes þrym
   205 geberan, beorhtne sunu,      bearn eacen godes,
        torhtes tirfruman.
```

'Gabriel,
the archangel of heaven, gave me greeting.
He told me truly that the heavenly spirit
would illumine me with radiance, that I should

bear life's glory, the glorious Son, the child of Almighty God,
the resplendent prince of glory.'

The lines refer directly to the Son, but the verbal correspondence
with passages where the reference was to the solar body makes its
connection with the pun all but inevitable.

Following almost immediately in the Passus we find:

> Nu þu ealle forlæt
> sare sorgceare.   Saga ecne þonc
> 210 mærum meotodes sunu   þæt ic his modor gewearð.

> 'You must forsake now all
> grevious sorrow. Give eternal thanks
> to the great Son of God that I have become His mother.'

It is significant that in other passages where the puns are made
they are associated directly with the exile figure. It is obviously
more difficult to deal with such images in a passage of dialogue;
however, although the images do not appear directly, the theme of
exile is certainly suggested, as has been pointed out by Greenfield.[10]
The Passus follows immediately the *O Emmanuel* passage with
its heavy emphasis upon the exiles in Limbo awaiting the harrowing, thus anticipating the eschatological theme of the final
section of the poem. The action of the Passus takes place in the
days shortly before the birth of Christ, when all men existed in
exile. Finally, the finger of scorn pointed at Joseph surely places
him in a position of exile from his fellowmen. The *O Rex Pacifice*
passage, following immediately, continues the emphasis upon the
exile pattern in its theme of the scattered flock.

As we bring the discussion of the first section of the poem to a
close, it should be pointed out, also, that Mary's reference to her-
self as the temple of God acts as a climax to the architectural
imagery which had its beginning in the reference to Christ as the
rejected wallstone. The stone rejected at the beginning has now
come to full fruition as the cornerstone of the temple of faith.

The second division of *Christ* begins with line 440. Greenfield
concluded his study of the pattern of exile at the end of Part I. I

---

[10] "The Theme of Spiritual Exile in Christ I", pp. 327ff.

shall pursue through the concluding two sections of the poem the
images not only of exile but also of Christ as the lock or key, the
nautical imagery, and the pattern of word-play. The figure of the
exile occurs with considerable frequency in Part II; the other
images occur only once each.

The image of the Holy City, mentioned as a minor motif in
Part I, becomes more important in Part II, occurring at lines 461b,
615b, and 534b, in each instance having its usual significance of
the City of God, the end of the Christian exile.

> 460   Sona wæron gearwe,
>   hæleð mid hlaford,   to þære halgan byrg.

> 'Soon they were made ready,
> the men with the Lord, for the Holy City.'

The image of the Holy City is particularly apt to the exile at this
point. It occurs at the point in time when the true meaning of the
exile is made apparent by Christ's order to the disciples to disperse
and spread His message throughout the lands. The Old Testament
exile as interpreted by the church fathers was in one important
aspect a prophecy of this very exile which began with the life and
death of Jesus. The difference between the conceptions of the exile
as expressed in the Old and New Testaments was, of course, that,
with the life and ministry of Jesus, the possibility of man's salvation had become a reality, a reality which existed only as a prophecy
in the Old Testament. The song of the angels after Christ's ascension
continues to emphasize the eschatological motif of the Holy City
with its references to Christ's native home, his *fæder eþelstoll*
(516b) and *þære beorhtan byrg* (519a).

The exile image which follows at line 481a and is a part of
Christ's order to the disciples gathered at the Ascension establishes
the connection between the two aspects of the theme, the Holy
City and the Christian exile:

> "Gefeoð ge on ferððe!   Næfre ic from hweorfe,
>   ac ic lufan symle   læste wið eowic,
>   ond eow meaht giefe   ond mid wunige,
>   awo to ealdre,   þæt eow æfre ne bið
> 480 þurh gife mine   godes onsien.

Farað nu geond ealne   yrmenne grund,
geond widwegas,   weoredum cyðcað."

' "Rejoice in spirit! Never shall I desert you,
but I shall show my love to you continually
and give you strength and live among you
forever and ever, that you, as a result of
my gift, may never be lacking of God.
Go now through all the wide earth,
the far-distant paths, proclaim to men." '

In these lines Christ proclaims the final phase of the Christian's
exile, a phase which is to end with His Second Advent. These lines
anticipate the final section of the poem, which is built on the theme
of the Judgment, when man will receive the final and full revelation of the meaning of his life of exile on earth. In the image of
the scattering of the disciples on their evangelical mission lies the
hope of the world, which will live in the Church and be revealed
at the Last Judgment. Whereas, at the Crucifixion, the world lay
palled in darkness, at the Ascension we have light and hope. The
frequent occurrence of images of whiteness and light in Part II
constitutes a significant part of this theme of hope.

There occurs in these lines what appears to be a pun which
points up the theological theme. Lines 479b-480, *þæt eow æfre
ne bið / þurh gife mine godes onsien*, may be translated either 'that
you, as a result of my gift, may never be lacking God', or 'that
you, as a result of my gift, may never be lacking sustenance'.[11]
The significance of the pun is, of course, that God is the sustenance
of the Christian; more specifically, that He is the gift of Jesus and
His life, and, at the Last Supper, the gift of His body and blood,
the sacrament of Holy Communion. This is the very gift that the
sufferers in the prison house, an image so prominent in the first
section of the poem, have been praying for and awaiting. The
images of exile, the gift of Jesus, and the Holy City encompass an
entire structure of the life of the Christian who accepts and fulfils
his commitment of faith.

[11] The Bosworth-Toller *Supplement*, pp. 478-479, translates *god* "something, material or non-material, that is of advantage". This suggestion of
the material seems to permeate the entry, in spite of references to spiritual
goods.

The reference to the Holy City at line 516b mentions that Christ has ascended to *fæder eþelstoll* 'the native land of the Father'. In line 519a, the phrase *þære beorhtan byrg* 'the shining city', occurs, calling attention not only to the figure of the city but also to the light imagery mentioned as a part of the theme of hope in Part II.

The lines describing the joy in heaven after the Ascension and the sad departure of the disciples toward Jerusalem give us both a literal and a figurative level of meaning.

>   Hyht wæs geniwad,
> 530 blis in burgum,   þurh þæs beornes cyme.
>   Gesæt sigehremig   on þa swiþran hand
>   ece eadfruma   agnum fæder.
>   Gewitan him þa gongan   to Hierusalem
>   hæleð hygerofe,   in þa halgan burg,
>   geomormode.

>   'Joy was renewed,
>   bliss in the cities, by the coming of the Son.
>   Triumphant, He sat on the right hand
>   of the true source of joy, His own Father.
>   Then the valiant men set out toward Jerusalem,
>   toward the holy city,
>   sad in spirit.'

On the literal level, the journey is the actual one, but on the figurative level, the setting out toward Jerusalem signifies the beginning of the final phase of the Christian exile, which is to be terminated in the City of God after the Last Judgment. The reference in line 530 to heaven as *burgum* indicates the naturalness with which the figure occurs in the context of earthly and heavenly extremes of home.

The only other significant reference to the city figure in Part II is not to the City of God or of earth but to the city of Satan. Such a 'city' was never a part of the conception of St. Augustine, who conceived of the duality of earthly and heavenly cities as the polarities of moral and spiritual existence, but the poet has broadened a universally accepted figure in order to express an entirely new conception of the exile theme. To be sure, the basis of this new expression of man's exile is in the Bible and in exegetical tradition,

but the poet has given to the idea a highly artistic treatment, typical
of the imaginative manner in which he handles his material. The
reference to the city occurs as part of a long passage which must
be quoted in full:

> Nu sind forcumene   ond in cwicsusle
> gehynde ond gehæfte,   in helle grund
> duguþum bidæled,   deofla cempan.
> Ne meahtan wiþerbrogan   wige spowan,
> 565 wæpna wyrpum,   siþþan wuldres cyning,
> heofonrices helm,   hilde gefremede
> wiþ his ealdfeondum   anes meahtum,
> þær he of hæfte ahlod   huþa mæste
> of feonda byrig,   folces unrim,
> þisne ilcan þreat   þe ge her on stariað.

> 'Now are they overcome and in living torment,
> humbled and bound in the deeps of hell,
> deprived of glory, warriors of the devil.
> Nor may the adversaries succeed in battle
> by casting weapons, because the King of Glory,
> the Ruler of heaven, made war
> against His ancient enemies by His single might,
> when He wrested unnumbered folk from bondage,
> from the city of fiends, this very band
> you gaze on here, the greatest of spoils.'

The opening three lines of the passage, describing the hopeless
condition of the damned in hell, make use of images which
resemble somewhat those describing the condition of the exiles in
Part I. I submit that this resemblance is exactly what the poet
intended and that he meant the resemblance to anticipate a
broader development of this new aspect of the exile theme, particularly in Part III. The new aspect is specifically the notion of
permanent exile from God's grace as a result of deliberate choice
of transient earthly joy instead of the permanent joy promised in
the life and ministry of Jesus. This new aspect of the exile is possible only after the earthly ministry of Jesus; therefore, it enters the
poem only after the Ascension has put the choice of salvation or
damnation squarely up to the Christian. There is now in the
thematic structure of the poem not only the earthly exile but also
the permanent exile which is hell itself. The figure of the city of

the fiends, an obvious contrast to the City of God, makes the point. Following the passage devoted to the development of the contrast comes a rhapsodic summation of the hope motif and with it another reference to man's life as an exile:

>   ... nu monna gehwylc
> 590 cwic þendan her wunað,   geceosan mot.
>
>   '... now each man,
>   while he lives here, must choose.'

The phrase *cwic þendan her wunað* implies the earthly exile. The choice is directly stated. True, man had exercised free choice in Eden, but never until after the Resurrection and Ascension had the meaning of the choice been so fully and brilliantly clear.

Immediately following this emphasis upon choice comes the first of the poet's uses of the word *wræce* in Part II. The use of the word is of particular significance here because it describes not the condition of the earthly exiles but that of the fiends permanently exiled in hell, and, specifically, it describes Satan himself. The lines in which the word occurs are the famous ones in which the poet uses the balanced, internally rhymed line. Such extensive use of rhyme occurs in only one other Old English poem, *The Rhyming Poem*. The balanced phrases set up and emphasize the choices open to man, one of which, ironically, is *þystra wræce* 'the pride of the wretched', line 593b.

>   ... nu monna gehwylc
> 590 cwic þendan her wunað,   geceosan mot
>   swa helle hienþu   swa heofones mærþu,
>   swa þæt leohte leoht   swa ða laþan niht,
>   swa þrymmes þræce   swa þystra wræce,
>   swa mid dryhten dream   swa mid deoflum hream,
>   swa wite mid wraþum   swa wuldor mid arum,
>   swa lif swa dead,   swa him leofre bið
>   to gefremmanne,   þenden flæsc ond gæst
>   wuniað in worulde.

The passage closes with the hortatory emphasis on the necessity for immediate action, an emphasis which has eschatological overtones. The choice points up again the importance of Christ's ministry to the life of man; it also anticipates the broad development in Part III of the motif of those permanently exiled in hell as a result of their failure to commit themselves to the life of the Christian exile. The commitment motif also recalls the distinction between the seafarer and the land-dweller, which will be suggested in the closing lines of Part II.

The poet then continues to develop, from lines 600–20, the notion of Christ as the deliverer of man from God's original punitive decree as stated at the expulsion from Eden. The lines emphasize sharply the distinction between the Old and the New Law and reemphasize the distinction, pointed out above, between the two conceptions of the exile, the Old Testament as prophetic of the New. Beginning with line 621, the poet recalls the expulsion as the beginning of man's exile and sets up Job as an example of the Old Testament situation. The flashback is important to the development of the theme. In the first place, it puts a specific emphasis upon the exile as a traditional figure for mortal man, and, second, it states specifically the interpretation of the Old Testament situation as prophetic of the New, thus carrying forward the emphasis upon the additional importance of the exile after the Crucifixion, Resurrection, and Ascension. At line 622b occurs a second use of the word *wræce*, this time in its usual significance of the hard lot of the earthly exile. God's order of expulsion is stated in the lines

"Ic þec ofer eorðan geworhte, on þære þu scealt yrmþum lifgan,
wunian in gewinne ond wræce dreogan."

' "I wrought you on the earth; on it you will live in want,
dwell in hostility, endure in exile." '

Line 633a again makes use of the word to describe the life of the earthly exile, but in this instance in a pun:

Bi þon giedd awræc Iob, swa he cuðe.
'Of this, Job composed a song, as well he could."

[The 'this' refers to Christ's wish to help the exiles, expressed in the preceding lines.] The verb *wrecan* means literally 'to utter' or 'to recite', but it is a perfect pun on the word *wræcca* or *wrecca* 'one driven from his own country', 'a wanderer in foreign lands', 'an exile', as we have seen in the discussion of the opening line of *The Wanderer.*

After the passage based on the 'leaps' of Christ, lines 720ff, there is a hortatory passage warning man to be on guard against the wiles of the devil:

> Utan us beorgan þa,
> 772 þenden we on eorðan   eard weardien.

> 'Let us then defend ourselves
> while we keep our home on earth.'

The reference to the necessity to defend oneself while on earth certainly refers to man in the condition of exile, in the theological context.

If we enter the signature passage at line 793b, we will find at 794a a use of the word *wræc* to describe the terror of possible damnation, and at line 799a as a reference to the exile of this world.

> Ic þæs brogan sceal
> geseon synwræce,   þæs þe ic soð talge,
> þær monig beoð   on gemot læded
> fore onsyne   eces deman.
> Þonne ·ᚻ· cwacað,   sprecan reþe word
> þam þe him ær in worulde   wace meahtan
> 800 þendan ·ᛗ· ond ·ᛉ·   yþast meahtan
> frofre findan.   Þær sceal forht monig
> on þam wongstede   werig bidan
> hwæt him æfter dædum   deman wille
> wraþra wita.   Biþ se ·ᚹ· scæcen
> eorþan frætwa.   ·ᚢ· wæs longe
> ·ᛚ· flodum bilocen,   lifwynna dæl,
> ·ᚠ· on foldan.

> 'I shall see terror
> in the punishments for sins, this I reckon truthfully;
> where many will be led all together
> into the sight of the Eternal Judge.
> The KEEN will quake when he hears the King in judgment,
> the just Ruler speak just words
> to those who obeyed Him but feebly before, in the world,
> when AFFLICTION and DISTRESS might have most easily
> found comfort. There, in that place, many
> will await in fear, sad at heart,

what dire punishment will be judged for them
for their deeds. Then will JOY
of earthly goods, OUR portion of life's pleasures,
all the POSSESSIONS of earth,
long locked in flood WATERS, flee.'

In making this translation I have referred to Gollancz's interpretation of the runes as given in his *The Exeter Book*. A lengthy discussion of the runes is also to be found in Cook's edition. I have not used Gollancz's translations exclusively, as is apparent, but since his interpretations seem to agree generally with those of other scholars in the field, I have used them when they fit my purpose.

We find the word *wræce* used in the signature passage in an unusual sense, to denote terror. Certainly the notion of terror is not foreign to the context of the Last Judgment, but we have not till now seen the poet associate terror with the condition of exile. The implication of terror is particularly apt here, however, when we remember that the exile theme has been shown to be moving through the poem to a climax in the permanent exile of the damned after the Last Judgment has been made. It is this terror of eternal exile from the love of God of which the Christian exile must be constantly aware if he is to avoid it. The phrase *in worulde* pinpoints the notion of the exile's life on earth, where his choice will anticipate the final choice to be made by the Eternal Judge. Cynewulf consistently uses his signature passages to bring home his theme. Since one aspect of his theme is always eschatological, the climax here at the end of the second section of the poem anticipates the development of the theme of judgment in the third and final section.

Following the signature passage is another hortatory passage in which men are urged to consider the meaning of mortality. Here occurs the final use in Part II of the exile figure.

> Forþon ic leofra gehwone   læran wille
> þæt he ne agæle   gæstes þearfe,
> ne on gylp geote,   þenden god wille
> þæt he her in worulde   wunian mote,
> somed siþian   sawel in lice,
> 820 in þam gæsthofe.

> 'Therefore, I wish to teach each loved one
> not to neglect the needs of the spirit
> nor pour it forth in boasts, the while that God wills
> that he live here in this world,
> journey together, soul and body,
> in this inn.'

The phrase *in worulde* is expanded in this passage by the images of the journey and the inn. Both of these images have been pointed out in numerous references to man's life as an exile, the journey suggesting the apparent endlessness, the inn the impermanence of the earthly dwelling place.

The final images in Part II which bear upon the theme of exile are the nautical images. These images occur in almost the final lines of the section, beginning at line 850. However, there is an image of water at line 806a which is highly significant. It occurs in the signature passage and involves the rune $\mathord{\vdash}$, generally taken to signify 'sea' or 'water'. The passage also contains an unusual use of the lock image. The juxtaposition of the images is paradoxical. The passage says that man's mortal portion is locked in flood waters. In the first place, we usually associate, in the allegorical tradition, mortal life with the sea, which association creates an apparent redundancy in the implication that man's mortal existence is limited by his mortal existence. Also, the placing of controlling power in man's mortal nature seems to violate the very heart of the thematic structure, which has made Christ the lock or controlling force in human life. How can we reconcile these difficulties? First, there is an irrefutable logic in the implication that mortality controls man's mortal existence. Such a theme is at the heart of the traditional dialogue between body and soul which appears throughout medieval literature. To say that man's spiritual existence is expressed by his mortal life and is therefore to a degree controlled by it is to indulge in the obvious. If this be so, the association of the lock image with the flood waters is explained, but we are left with a confusing unexplained associaton – that of Christ and the flood waters, via the lock image. The association is to be explained, it seems to me, by the dual nature of Christ and His ministry, the material and the spiritual. It is the poet's insistence that Christ is to be seen as a controlling force in our mortal as well as our spiritual existences, that, in fact, He must control our mortality in order to fulfil His dual nature as the controlling force in the whole man. To the Christian, Christ must control man's earthly exile in order to make possible man's salvation. Christ is the key who will free man from the power of sin and temptation by opening the doors of man's earthly prison, just as He is the key who will eventually open to man the gates to paradise or to hell. Thus, man is controlled not only by his mortality, or perhaps not really by his mortality at all, in the ultimate sense, but by the power of the dual nature of Christ as a recognized part of his mortal existence. Seen in this light, there is a startling subtlety to the statement that our allotted portion of life's joy has long been locked in the flood waters of our mortal existence. Such a theme is intensified by the sense of the impending end added by the eschatological images.

The image is even further intensified by its suggestion of an unrealized power in the hold over man of the goods and glories of the world. It suggests perhaps a depth of man's commitment to these pleasures which will not be realized or admitted until too late, until the admission is forced upon man at the Last Judgment. The image of the flood-lock recalls the treasures of the Egyptians which were dashed forever in the depths of the Red Sea, locked in death forever by the power of God in the depths of the Egyptians' worldly pursuits, but which floated to the surface to be reclaimed as God's true spiritual goods by the Israelites on the far shore of their commitment to their exile, which they had accepted as their part in the covenant made between God and Abraham.

The image of flood waters takes on even more significance when, just 43 lines later, we find the lengthy elaboration of man's exile as a sea voyage:

850   Nu is þon gelicost   swa we on laguflode
      ofer cald wæter   ceolum liðan
      geond sidne sæ,   sundhengestum,
      flodwudu fergen.   Is þæt frecne stream
      yða ofermæta   þe we her on lacað
      geond þas wacan woruld,   windge holmas
      ofer deop gelad.   Wæs se drohtað strong
      ærþon we to londe   geliden hæfdon

ofer hreone hrycg.   Þa us help bicwom,
þæt us to hælo   hyþe gelædde,
860 godes gæstsunu,   ond us giefe sealde
þæt we oncnawan magnun   ofer ceoles bord
hwær we sælan sceolon   sundhengestas,
ealde yðmearas,   ancrum fæste.
Utan us to þære hyðe   hyht staþelian,
ða us gerymde   rodera waldend,
halge on heahþu,   þa he heofonum astag.

'Now it is most like as if we fare in ships
over the flood, sail in sea-steeds over the cold
water, far over the flood paths. It is a perilous
stream of immeasurable waves over which we toss
here in this feeble world, led over the deep,
the windy expanse of sea. The way was difficult before
we were brought to land over the savage ridges of
wave. Then help came to us, God's Spirit-Son, and
gave to us grace that we on ship-board might know
where we should moor fast with anchors the sea-steeds,
the ancient wave-horses. Let us fix our hope to this
haven which the Master of the skies opened to us,
holiness on high, when He rose to heaven.'

The images of the ship and sea and sailor are all familiar to the reader of Old English religious poetry. The four motifs which I mentioned at the beginning of the discussion of this section of the poem were those of exile, Christ as the lock, nautical imagery, and word-play. All of these motifs are brought to a climactic cluster-point in these final lines of Part II. The sea journey is the exile. The association of Christ, the lock, with water imagery was forcefully made in the signature passage, which association is recalled here in the nautical imagery. The word-play has centered on *sunu*, which is tied in with the reference to the Spirit-Son. The final words of the section are a petition that all Christians might find hope in the Son. The artistic power of the passage speaks eloquently for itself.

It should be noted that the elegiac tone in these lines is almost exactly the tone of the sea passages in *The Wanderer* and *The Seafarer*. It is such similarity of tone that has led to much of the speculation concerning influence of one poem or poet upon another.

However, if what I have been suggesting here about the nature of Old English poetry and the relationship between theme and imagic pattern is true, it seems highly likely that the influence is not so much that of poems or poets upon each other as that of the entire medieval background of patristic writings and exegesis upon the Old English poetic tradition in its entirety.

The final section of the poem is 797 lines in length, almost as long as Parts I and II combined. In it we find all the thematic motifs which made up the structure of the earlier parts except that of nautical imagery. The image of the exile appears more than 20 times, making use toward the end of the poem of the inn house figure. This number of appearances is greater than in the first two parts combined, and in Part III it takes on a new and significant aspect. The figure of Christ as the lock comes to a meaningful climax in Part III, and the play on the word *sunu* continues throughout. Finally, we shall see a significant pattern of use of the word *wræc* or its derivatives. I shall comment only generally on the images of light and dark, which the poet uses to support the thematic patterns of God's glory and man's sin and the contrast between salvation and damnation in the Last Judgment. The disappearance of the nautical imagery is consonant with the thematic development. The first two sections of the poem have turned upon the contrast between those men who accept their roles as Christian exiles (seafarers) and those who knowingly reject such a role (land-dwellers), but now that the theme of contrast is to be resolved, the nautical imagery is no longer apropos.

The change in significance of the exile theme is the most important thematic development of Part III. Two new meanings of exile become apparent. First, as has been anticipated, the notion of exile moves in time and in moral suggestion from the literal, tropological, and allegorical levels to the specifically anagogical; second, exile becomes associated with Christ's acceptance of His earthly ministry. We shall see how these changes in the suggestion of the images bring to a conclusion the theme of exile in the poem as a whole.

The central figure of the exile enters the third section at line 956 and here establishes its anagogical use:

Þær mægen werge monna cynnes
wornum hweorfað on widne leg,
þa þær cwice meteð cwelmende fyr,
sume up, sume niþer, ældes fulle.
960 Þonne bið untweo þæt þær Adames
cyn, cearena full, cwiþeð gesarad.

'Then the great cursed horde of mankind
will be turned forth to wander here and there
in spreading flame, in crowds of men,
where the living will meet engulfing fire.
Then it will certainly come to pass that Adam's
kin, full of sorrow, will lament, afflicted.'

Before discussing the exile figure, we should note the pun on the word *mægen*. Although the literal meaning in context is probably 'horde' or 'host', the word carries another denotation, 'force', which serves a double meaning in this syntactic slot. The word 'force' can denote a body of men, but it can also mean power or capacity. At the Last Judgment, the power of man to pervert good to evil will get its just due by being exiled into eternal damnation. Here, we have the shift in the use of exile to suggest the permanent exile from God's love. The exile motif is strengthened by the reference to man as the kin of Adam, the first exile, and to the notion of wandering implied in the construction *wornum hweorfað ... sume up, sume niþer*, here an eternal wandering the paths of exile in hell, from which there is no hope of salvation. The poet has brought together here the cluster of suggestions in order to make the point of the thematic development which will dominate Part III.

Lines 1298–99 continue the emphasis on wandering:

Þær hi ascamode, scondum gedreahte,
swiciað on swiman.

'There they, ashamed, afflicted with disgrace,
wander giddily.'

It is to be noted that the damned wander 'giddily', that is to say, aimlessly, hopelessly, which was, ironically, the condition of man before the First Advent.

The following lines are part of a long passage describing the coming of Christ to the Judgment:

1040   Micel ariseð
     dryhtfolc to dome,   sibþan deaþes bend
     toleseð liffruma.   Lyft við onbærned,
     hreosað heofonsteorran,   hyþað wide
     gifre glede,   gæstas hweorfað
     on ecne eard.

                    'A great multitude
     will arise to judgment, after the bonds of death
     have been loosed by the Author of Life. The heavens will be
     the stars of heaven will fall, the greedy flame   kindled,
     will lay wide waste, spirits will return to
     their eternal home.'

The two images important to the exile pattern here are those of
bonds and of the eternal home. The notion that the exile is bound
to the mortal hardships of his path is here given its ultimate significance in the stated release from earthly bonds, and, further, by
the assured entry into some form of eternity. The loosing from
bonds and the opening for the faithful of the way to the City of
God recalls directly the function of Christ as the key or lock. The
release through and from death is, of course, the necessary step in
the progress toward the eternal reward. The association of bonds
with exile is also to be recalled in the elegies and in *Exodus*.

In the context of the Judgment, we have, at line 1075, a
reference to the earthly home:

                    Wile fæder eahtan
     hu gesunde suna   sawle bringen
1075 of þam eðle   þe hi on lifdon.

                    'The Father will judge
     how, all sound, His sons will bring their souls
     from the home where they have lived.'

The *eðle* in which the sons have lived is certainly the earth on
which they have endured their mortal exile. The word shares the
meaning here, also, of the heavenly home, the goal of exile.

The increasing complexity of levels of meaning on which the
exile figure is used in Part III is exemplified by the poet's bringing
into the thematic motif all the image structures which have
appeared in the poem. That these figures are brought deliberately

into the exile theme indicates the primacy of the theme to the poet's conception of his structure. A passage beginning at line 1255 introduces the lock image:

> Đonne hi þy geornor   gode þonciað
> blædes ond blissa   þe hy bu geseoð,
> þæt he hy generede   from niðcwale
> ond eac forgeaf   ece dreamas;
> bið him hel bilocen,   heofonrice agiefen.

> 'Then they will the more eagerly thank God
> for the blessings and the gladness when they see that He both
> delivered them from hateful torment
> and also gave to them eternal joys;
> to them hell will be locked, heaven's kingdom given.'

The lines come at the end of the passage describing the three signs which will manifest to the blessed their state of grace. The signs will tell them that they are saved from the torments of the damned because they have fulfilled their obligations to God and man. The door to hell is locked to them; they will not enter there.

The first use of the word *wræc* in part III occurs at line 1271a.

> An is þara   þæt hy him yrmþa to fela,
> grim helle fyr,   gearo to wite
> 1270 ondweard seoð,   on þam hi awo sculon,
> wræc winnende,   wærgðu dreogan.

> 'One of these is that they will see before them
> too many miseries, grim hell fire ready to torment them,
> in which they will forever endure damnation,
> suffering wretchedly.'

The word is a pun here, as it is on numerous occasions in such a context. It means both 'exile' and 'wretchedness'. The lines describe the first of the three sources of torment for the damned. Being described here is the realization of the damned that they have earned permanent exile from God's grace. The play on *wræc* fits meaning perfectly.

The following lines close the long passage which describes the sorrows of those rejected from salvation:

> Ne þæt ænig mæg   oþrum gesecgan
> mid hu micle elne   æghwylc wille

þurh ealle list   lifes tiligan,
   feores forhtlice,   forð aðolian,
1320 synrust þwean   ond hine sylfne þrean,
   ond þæt wom ærran   wunde hælan,
   þone lytlan fyrst   þe her lifes sy,
   þæt he mæge fore eagum   eorðbuendra
   unscomiende eðles mid monnum
   brucan bysmerleas,   þendan bu somod
   lic ond sawle   lifgan mote.

'No one can tell another
with what great zeal each desires,
desperately, by means of any art, to obtain life,
to wash out the foulness of sin,
to endure, and to chasten himself,
and thereby to heal the wound of former evil,
during the little space of life that is here,
so that he may, before the eyes of the earth-dwellers,
unshamedly have blameless enjoyment
of his home among men, while
both body and soul abide together.'

The lines contain three specific suggestions of the exile theme.
First, the eschatological suggestion of line 1322 emphasizes the
need to prepare while there is time. Second, the *eorðbuendra* of
line 1323 are the land-dwellers who are always contrasted with the
truly committed Christian exile as seafarer. Third, the body-and-
soul-together motif is hortatory, suggesting the impermanence of
the mortal state, *þendan bu somod / lic ond sawle lifgan mote.*
Another point of interest in these lines is in the suggestion that the
true Christian appears blameless in the eyes of men. At first there
seems something distastefully sanctimonious in the idea, but the
lines perhaps suggest the Augustinian contrast between enjoyment
and use. Enjoyment of a thing, says St. Augustine, for its own sake
is evil. The only true enjoyment we have in a particular thing, he
says, is in making use of it to strive for a higher happiness. It is
this state of true enjoyment that the Christian must attempt to
present to his fellow man if he is to live as an example of true
Christian love and commitment.
    Beginning at line 1379 we have God's anticipated speech to

sinners at the Judgment, in which He recalls the expulsion from
the Garden in lines 1403ff.:

> ða þu of þan gefean   fremde wurde,
> feondum to willan   feor aworpen.
> Neorxnawonges wlite   nyde sceoldes
> agiefen geomormod,   gæsta eþel,
> earg ond unrot,   eallum bidæled
> dugeþum ond dreamum,   ond þa bidrifen wurde
> on þas þeostran weoruld,   þær þu þolades siþþan
> 1410 mægenearfeþu   micle stunde,
> sar ond swar gewin   ond sweartne deað.

> 'Then you became alien to that gladness,
> to the delight of fiends, cast afar out.
> You then sadly but assuredly gave up
> the perfection of paradise, the home of the spirit,
> deprived of all blessings and joys,
> wretched and sorrowful; and then were you driven
> into this dark world where you have suffered
> since great and enduring hardship,
> sorrow and grief and swarthy death.'

Traditionally in patristic writing the expulsion was the beginning
of man's exile, an interpretation which became more strongly en-
trenched during the Middle Ages, as witness the many references
to fallen man as 'the race of Adam'. The phrase occurs numerous
times in both *Christ* and *Exodus*. The above passage contains many
images associated with the exile theme: the loss of paradise, the
dark world into which the wretched one is cast, the sufferings and
hardships, the necessity of death. The Old Testament emphasis on
suffering is to be noted, an emphasis which was to be alleviated
by the birth of Christ and His ministry.

The concluding lines of God's anticipated address to the sinful
ones are

>   "Eall ge þæt me dydan,
> to hynþum heofoncyninge.   Þæs ge sceolon hearde adreogan
> wite to widan ealdre,   wræc mid deoflum geþolian."

>   ' "All this you did to Me,
> in contempt of the King of Heaven. For that you will forever
> suffer hard punishment, endure exile with the devils." '

In the lines, we hear Christ speaking through God and giving the Christian culmination to the expulsion by carrying it through the Second Advent. This conception of the exile theme will develop into the great recapitulation scene of the finale.

The image of the inn house enters the exile theme at line 1535:

1530   Swapeð sigemece   mid þære swiðran hond
    þæt on þæt deope dæl   deofol gefeallað
    in sweartne leg,   synfulra here
    under foldan sceat,   fæge gæstas
    on wraþra wic,   womfulra scolu
    werge to forwyrde   on witehus,
    deaðsele deofles.

    'He will sweep with the victory mace in His right hand
    the devils tumbling into the deep pit,
    into swarthy flame, the horde of sinful
    fated spirits under the place of sepulchre,
    into the den of evil ones, howling,
    damned to perdition in the house of torment,
    the death-hall of the devil.'

The house image recalls similar figures, such as *gæsthofe* (820a) and *carcerne* (25b), figures which are used traditionally to indicate earthly exile and to emphasize the transient and oppressive character of mortality. The word *witehus* operates on a highly ironic level, carrying over from life into death the suffering of the unfaithful, suggesting that for the unfaithful there is no end to exile. These same notions are repeated over and over again in the concluding lines of Part III. Line 1617 says specifically that on the Day of Judgment the unfaithful will *from his scyppende ascyred weorðan*. The image of hell as a house appears at 1603b, *susla hus,* at 1624a, *helle biluceð / morþerhusa mæst*, and at 1627b, *þæt is dreamleas hus.* At line 1639, heaven is called *se eþel þe no geendad weorþeð*, stating that heaven will be the end of exile for the faithful.

The motif of the ministry of Christ as part of the exile pattern of Part III finds its most significant statement beginning at line 1420b:

1420   Wearð ic ana geboren
    folcum to frofre.   Mec mon folmum biwond,

biþeahte mid þearfan wædum,   ond mec þa on þeostre alegde
biwundenne mid wonnum claþum.   Hwæt, ic þæt for
                                                                                worulde geþolade!
Lytel þuhte ic leoda bearnum,   læg ic on heardum stane,
cildgeong on crybbe.   Mid þy ic þe wolde cwealm afyrran,
hat helle bealu,   þæt þu moste halig scinan
eadig on þam ecan life,   forðon ic þæt earfeþe wonn.
     Næs me for mode,   ac ic on magugeoguðe
yrmþu geæfnde,   arleas licsar,
þæt ic þurh þa   wære þe gelic.

                      'I was born alone,
as a comfort to men. They wrapped me with their hands
in wretched cloths, in paupers' rags, and laid me in darkness.
This I suffered for the world!
Men thought little of me; I lay on hard stone,
a baby in a crib. By means of this,
because I suffered this degredation, I saved you from death,
from the depravity of hot hell, so that you might shine most
happy in eternal life.   holy,
     It was not because of pride, just so I could be like you,
that I, a youth, bore this disgrace,
the misery of death.'

The words of the passage are highly suggestive of mortality and
suffering, words such as *biwond, biwundenne, þeostre, geþolade,
geæfnde, arleas, licsar.* That God should describe His coming to
earth in terms suggesting the mortal condition is orthodox theologically, but in the context of the poetic structure the meanings
recall the exiled condition of man. God seems to be saying here
that He will suffer exile Himself, exile from His own bliss, in order
to be a man, not just as a meaningless act of pride, but as an act of
redemption. The passage continues for another 34 lines in words
that liken the body of Christ to the body of mortal man and emphasize man's mistreatment of Christ during His exile on earth.
     This passage recalls a shorter one at lines 1171ff. describing the
life of Christ on earth:

                            . . . þær he earfeþu
geþolade fore þearfe   þeodbuendra,
laðlicne deað   leodum to helpe.

                      '. . . where He bore

suffering, loathsome death, to help man,
for the profit of earth's inhabitants.'

Words either identical with those of the later passage or having similar meaning pinpoint the motif of mortal suffering, degradation, and death: *earfeþu, geþolade, laðlicne.* The lines add to the significance of God's life as man and His suffering as a man for the sake of man.

A third passage, at lines 1495–96, carry the theme farther:

> Ic wæs on worulde wædla þæt þu wurde welig in heofonum,
> earm ic wæs on eðle þinum þæt þu wurde eadig on minum.

'I was poor in this world so you could be rich in heaven,
I was wretched in your home so you could be happy in mine.'

The balanced antitheses sharpen the impact of the ironic message of God's voluntary suffering.

It seems to me that this new aspect of the exile theme illustrates the poet's deftness in adding complexity to his theme as he approaches the climax of the poem. The final irony of the human situation, as has been pointed out elsewhere, is that this man who came and suffered for men will be the one to return and judge man's dedication to His example at the Last Judgment.

There are three instances in Part III of the poem where the play on *sunu* has been used to sharpen the theme. The first instance occurs at line 900:

> Þonne semninga on Syne beorg
> 900 suþaneastan sunnan leoma
> cymeð of scyppende scynan leohtor
> þonne hit men mægen modum ahycgan,
> beorhte blican, þonne bearn godes
> þurh heofona gehleodu hider oðyweð.

> 'Then suddenly on Mount Sion
> there will come from the southeast
> a sunbeam from the Creator, shining more brightly
> than man can imagine,
> gleaming brightly, when the Son of God
> will appear through the vault of the heavens.'

The phrase *sunnan leoma* appeared several times in the first two sections of the poem, and in each instance it was shown that a sig-

nificant pun on *sunu* was almost certainly intended. The fact that
the sunbeam in the above passage comes from the Creator and
shines more brightly than man can imagine strengthens the
probability of the pun, particularly since the association of light
with God's truth is a universal symbolic significance. The final
lines of the passage state explicitly that this sunbeam will appear
when the Son appears in the heavens at the Last Judgment. One
more point might be made concerning the passage. According to
St. Augustine, it was traditional to associate Mt. Sion with contemplation.[12] The idea of contemplation is certainly to be associated
with the Last Judgment, at which time the universal intelligence
is to be seen in its final glory.

The following lines present a particularly difficult use of the
figure:

	Þæs he eftlean wile
1100 þurh eorneste	ealles gemonian,
ðonne sio reade	rod ofer ealle
swegle scineð	on þære sunnan gyld.

'For that He will
certainly exact a stern recompense,
when the red rood shines over all
in the heavens in place of the sun.'

On the literal level the meaning is clear. At the Last Judgment, the
Cross will shine over the world in place of the sun; the spirit will
replace the material source of light or life. However, if the pun on
sunnan is here, then it would seem that the rood is replacing the
Son at the Last Judgment. Such a reading, of course, clashes with
the usual sense we associate with the biblical narrative. The figurative sense of the lines, however, admits a wider possibility of interpretation. If the poet here means to elevate the Cross and the
Passion to an anagogical level of importance, in effect of higher
importance than that of the tropological level of the Son Himself
as man, he in effect places the act of His Passion at the very heart
of the meaning of Judgment. Such an interpretation seems to me

[12] St. Augustine, *Saint Augustine on the Psalms*, in: *Ancient Christian
Writers*, trans. and ed. by Dame Scholastica Hebgin and Dame Felicitas
Corrigan (London, 1960), p. 26.

theologically defensible. Although Christ's life and ministry were important as such, the central meaning of His earthly existence lies in His Passion and Resurrection. The great symbol involved in these acts, of course, is the Cross, and the acts themselves proved His divine nature. The Passion and the Resurrection, as discussed earlier, placed squarely upon the shoulders of man the responsibility for his own salvation, which, before Christ, had been impossible. Hence, the centrality of the Rood to the meaning of the Last Judgment.

There is also in the passage an interesting play on the word *gyld*, at line 1102b. *Gild*, of which *gyld* is a variant form, has a number of meanings, among which are 'a tribute', 'a substitution', 'a visible object of worship', 'a retribution'. It seems to me that all of these ideas work in the line. The notion of tribute, in the sense of veneration, is certainly associated with both Christ and the Cross, and the idea of substitution is emphasized in standard translations, such as those of Gollancz and R. K. Gordon.[13] The 'visible object of worship', however, is literally to be associated more with the Cross than with Christ, since an object suggests an inanimate thing. The line could be translated 'in place of the body of the sun'. The notions of veneration and retribution seem to go together to form an inviting ironic possibility in the situation of man standing before the throne of Judgment.

There can be little question of the significance of lines 1132b–33a, which describe the death on the Cross:

> Sunne wearð adwæsced,
> þream aþrysmed.

> 'The sun was darkened,
> stifled by sufferings.'

In these lines the spiritual and physical conditions of man and

---

[13] Gollancz, in *The Exeter Book*, Pt. I, p. 69, gives "when through all heaven, yea, instead of the sun / the red rood shall shine forth". Gordon, *Anglo-Saxon Poetry*, p. 169, gives "when the red cross shines brightly over all in place of the sun". Jacobus de Voragine cites St. John Chrysostom's statement that at the Last Judgment "The Cross and the Wounds will shine more brightly than the rays of the sun." See *The Golden Legend*, trans. and adapted by Granger Ryan and Helmut Ripperger (New York, 1941), I, 5.

earth are beautifully brought together. There is a possible difficulty in the lines in the suggestion that the life of Christ was stifled in His death. I submit that the lines ironically suggest the attitude of mind of or the effect on the lives of those responsible for the Crucifixion, the ironic tragedy of which is that it will prove their undoing rather than the undoing of Christ. In fact, the irony is even greater than this, since instead of undoing Christ's influence they have provided Him with the only means of proving His divinity – the Resurrection. It is the resurrected Christ who will appear at the Last Judgment to condemn those and all other sinners to the eternal exile of hell.

It is significant that at the end of this section describing the effect on creation of the Crucifixion we have the all-important repetition of the image of Christ as the stone, with which the fragmentary opening begins. The lines recall the Old Testament prophecy

1190   Þæt æt ærestan
      foreþoncle men   from fruman worulde
      þurh wis gewit,   witgan dryhtnes,
      halge higegleawe,   hæleþum sægdon,
      oft, nales æne,   ymb þæt æþele bearn,
      ðæt se earcnanstan   eallum sceolde
      to hleo ond to hroþer   hæleþa cynne
      weorðan in worulde,   wuldres agend,
      eades ordfruma,   þurh þa æþelan cwenn.

                              'That in the beginning
      wise, holy, and high-minded sages,
      men of the Lord, told men
      more than once, that the noble child,
      the precious stone, would come for all,
      would come through the noble queen,
      a refuge and a comfort to mankind,
      a wondrous lord, an origin of blessedness.'

Here is the blessed stone which the builders would reject from the wall but which would prove to be the cornerstone of the true temple. The prophecy is also a significant structural element in the poem if we recall a similar passage in the first section, beginning with line 60.

Only the figure of the lock remains to be discussed in any detail. The use of the image at line 1259a has already been noted, where hell is locked at the Judgment. There is another use of the figure at line 1055a, in the long passage which begins at 1040, describing the laying waste of the world after Christ has loosed men from the bonds of death:

> Ne bið þær wiht forholen
>   monna gehygda,   ac se mære dæg
> 1055 hreþerlocena hord,   heortan geþohtas,
>   ealle ætyweð.

> 'Not one bit of man's pride
> will be concealed on that great day,
> but all of the breast-locked horde of man's thoughts
> will be revealed.'

In this context, it seems reasonable to insist on a literal translation of *hreþerlocena*. Merely a dozen lines above we have had the use of the bond image, with Christ, as the key, loosing the bonds. It is usual to think of man's revealing his deepest locked secrets on the final day. The image of the lock and key fits the entire passage.

The final images of the lock occur, significantly, in the closing lines of the poem:

> Earm bið se þe wile
>   firenum gewyrcan,   þæt he fah scyle
>   from his scyppende   ascyred weorðan
>   æt domdæge   to deaðe niþer,
>   under helle cinn   in þæt hate fyr,
> 1620 under liges locan,   þær hy leomu ræcað
>   to bindenne   ond to bearnenne
>   ond to swingenne   synna to wite.
>   Ðonne halig gæst   helle biluceð,
>   morþerhusa mæst,   þurh meaht godes,
>   fyres fulle,   ond feonra here,
>   cyninges worde.

> 'He who desires to sin
> will be helpless; the guilty will
> at the Day of Doom be cut away
> from his Creator into deep death,
> shut into the race of hell in hot fire,
> locked in flame, his limbs stretched

to be bound, to be burned,
to be scourged in punishment for sin.
Then will the Holy Ghost lock up hell,
the greatest of murder houses, by the might of God, the word
full of fire and hordes of fiends.'   of the King,

The final act in dealing with the unfaithful will be the consigning
of them to their permanent exile in hell. The door will be locked
forever upon them. Here, for the first time in the poem, it is the
Holy Ghost who performs the act of locking. That the Holy Spirit,
the symbol of the consummate strength of the Holy Trinity, co-
existent with the Father and the Son, should perform the final act
of locking the gates of hell upon the damned is a fitting climax
to the poem. Just as baptism in the name of the Holy Ghost can
be made only after the Son is manifest, so damnation at Judgment.

There is one other interesting point in the passage. The word
leomu, line 1620b, bears what may be a significant resemblance
to *leoma*, a word which is used several times, at lines 106b, 696b,
and 900b in the phrase *sunnan leoma*, and at 234a in the phrase
leoma leohtade, in connection with the Son as a beam of light. If
the pun is intended, it has a peculiar richness in this context of
the damned locked forever in hell, since *ræcað* can be translated
'they will reach'. Here, for a moment in the description of the condition of the damned we are reminded of the possibility of their
having reached for the Lord, as, perhaps, they would now, had
they the opportunity once again. But then follow the resounding
parallel phrases *to bindenne, ond to bearnenne / ond to swingenne*,
and the fleeting memory is lost in the swarthy smoke and misery
of hell.

As I said at the beginning, the pattern of light and dark imagery
pervades the entire section with its obvious contrast between the
darkness of sin and the hope of grace. To attempt to deal with
these images in detail would take as much space as I have devoted
to the third section in its entirety.

In emphasizing the pattern of images relating to Christian exile,
including the associated figures of seafarers, land-dwellers, nautical
images, locks, keys, stones, inn houses, isolation generally, and
puns, I have not meant to imply that I have developed the only

reasonable way to read the poem *Christ*. I have tried to show, since these image patterns play an important part in what many scholars still regard as three separate poems, that there may be more reason than hitherto recognized for considering the material as a unit and thereby possibly by a single author, Cynewulf.

Themes of medieval poems tend to be statements of general and universally held attitudes, didactic, if you like. This is so perhaps because the period was one in which there was a wider unity of attitude than exists today concerning those things closest to the soul of man. This is not to say that there were not those who questioned deeply or even blatantly defied certain practices or prejudices of the time; it is to say that even such divergent types as Wyclif, Chaucer's Miller, or the irrepressible Sir Thomas Malory would probably never have considered the possibility of denying eternal verities. Modern man is much the same, except that modern man has shifted his notion of what constitutes eternal verities, via mass media and his mobility, from faith in a relevant future to faith in an immediacy, in which immediacy his most profound notion of unity seems to be his deceptive public stance that he will have none of it. Underneath is the same yearning for peace and stability but translated into a new sort of blatant defiance, into an individuality which, since it denies the individual, becomes not stability but a desperate clinging to the false felicity of earthly brotherhood.

Medieval poems usually found their themes, especially if they were religious poems, in patristic writing and exegesis, particularly among the great store of homilies and sermons. Since the poetry dealt with here has been religious poetry and since the sources of the poems are generally agreed upon as found in the religious writing of the period, there can be little doubt, it would follow, that their themes are religious. The point being made is that in the poetry of the early Middle Ages careful study is sure to discover many traditional image patterns and motifs which fill out and give strength to the more inclusive general themes of the poems. These images have been used by the poet to provide the details with which he makes his poem realistic and more complex. In fact, such details are the very stuff of his art, his realism, a fact which is so in any age. The medieval poet, after all, is an artist in the same way that a poet of the twentieth or any other century is an artist, a fact generally overlooked by scholars and critics who are willing to take the intellectual short-cut of dismissing the art of an earlier age as 'primitive' or 'crude' or both. We must remember that the pejorative sense of the word 'primitive' is a product of our culture. The Beowulf-poet, the poet of the Old English elegies, Caedmon, Cynewulf, the Pearl-poet, Chaucer, Malory, Shakespeare have all suffered from this kind of critical laziness. If the Old English poet had not been a competent artist, his poems would have been no more than paraphrases of the Scripture or the homilies, or copies of the saints' lives which served as their sources, but it is apparent that they are much more. Without the figure of the wanderer or the seafarer from the background of Germanic comitatus culture, the great religious impact of the poems which have been given the names of these figures might well have been lost, had the poems ever been written, but the presence of the figure cannot be used to argue against the religious theme. That the poems exist and are still read today is evidence not so much of the diligence of teachers as to the accomplishment of the poet-artists who created the symbolic figures from the popular cultural types. Such statements should not need the saying, and if we were speaking of poetry of a later age, they would not; however, of early medieval poetry such statements cannot be made often or loud enough. The work of the scholars and critics mentioned here is opening an entirely new aspect of the relationship between a writer, his time, his message, and his reader.

BIBLIOGRAPHY

An Anglo-Saxon Dictionary, based on the manuscript collections of the late Joseph Bosworth, edited and enlarged by J. Northcote Toller (London, 1954).

Anderson, George K., *The Literature of the Anglo-Saxons* (Princeton, 1949).

Anderson (Arngart), O. S., *The Seafarer: An Interpretation* (Lund, 1937).

Anonymous, "De Iona", in *The Ante-Nicene Fathers*, eds. the Rev. Alexander Roberts and James Donaldson (American Reprint of the Edinburgh Edition), 10 vols. (Grand Rapids, 1956).

Arnold, Thomas, *Beowulf: A Heroic Poem of the Eighth Century, with a Translation, Notes, and Appendix* (London, 1876).

Augustine, Saint, *On Christian Doctrine*, trans. D. W. Robertson, Jr. (New York, 1958).

——, *Concerning the Teacher* (De Magistro), trans. G. C. Leckie, in *Basic Writings of Saint Augustine*, ed. Whitney J. Oates (New York, 1948).

Baugh, Albert C., *A History of the English Language*, 2nd ed. (New York, 1957).

Bede, *Ecclesiastical History of England*, ed. J. A. Giles (London, 1849).

——, *A History of the English Church and People*, trans. Leo Sherley-Price (Baltimore, 1955).

Blackburn, F. A., ed., *Exodus and Daniel* (Boston, 1907).

——, "Is the 'Christ' of Cynewulf a Single Poem?", *Anglia*, XIX (1897), 88-98.

Blackman, E., Rev. of O. S. Anderson (Arngart), "*The Seafarer: An Interpretation*", *MLR*, XXXIV (1939), 254-255.

Boer, R. C., "Wanderer und Seefahrer", *ZfdP*, XXXV (1903), 1-28.

Bowen, E. G., *Settlements of the Celtic Saints in Wales* (Cardiff, 1954).

Brandl, Alois, "Englische Literatur: Angelsachsische Periode", *Grundriss der germanische Philologie*, ed. H. Paul, 2nd ed. (Strassburg, 1908).

Brewer, D. S., "Wanderer, Lines 50-57", *MLN*, XLVII (1952), 398-399.

Bright, James W., "The Relation of the Caedmonian *Exodus* to the Liturgy", *MLN*, XXVII (1912), 97-103.

Brooke, Stopford A., *English Literature from the Beginning to the Norman Conquest* (London, 1926).

Burgert, Edward, *The Dependence of Part I of Cynewulf's Christ on the Antiphonary* (Washington, D.C., 1921).

Burlin, Robert B., *The Old English Advent: A Typological Commentary* (New Haven, 1968).

Campbell, J. J., *The Advent Lyrics of the Exeter Book* (Princeton, 1959).

Cathcart, William, *The Ancient British and Irish Churches* (Philadelphia, 1894).

Chambers, R. W., *Beowulf, an Introduction*, 3rd ed. with a supplement by C. L. Wrenn (Cambridge, 1959).

Chrysostom, Saint John, *Commentary on Saint John the Apostle and Evangelist, Homilies 1-47*, Sister Thomas Aquinas Goggin. V. 33 of *The Fathers of the Church*, 72 vols. (New York, 1947-   ).

——, *Homilies on the Acts of the Apostles and the Epistle to the Romans*, V. 11 of *Nicene and Post-Nicene Fathers*, 1st ser., ed. Philip Schaff (Grand Rapids, 1956).

——, *Homily LX on the Gospel of St. John*, in V. 14 of *Nicene and Post-Nicene Fathers*, 1st ser., ed. Philip Schaff (Grand Rapids, 1956).

——, *Homily XXVIII on the Gospel of St. Matthew*, in V. 10 of *Nicene and Post-Nicene Fathers*, 1st ser., ed. Philip Schaff (Grand Rapids, 1956).

Commodian, *The Instructions of Commodianus in Favor of Christian Discipline*, trans. Robert Ernest Wallis, in *The Ante-Nicene Fathers*, 10 vols., eds. the Rev. Alexander Roberts and James Donaldson, Rev. A. Cleveland Coxe and Allan Menzies (Grand Rapids, 1968).

Cook, Albert S., "Greek Parallels to Certain Features of the *Beowulf*", *PQ*, V (1926), 226-234.

——, ed., *The Christ of Cynewulf* (Boston, 1909).

Courthope, W. J., *History of English Poetry*, 6 vols. (New York, 1885).

Cross, James E., "On the Genre of The Wanderer", *Neophil.*, XLV (1961), 63-72.

—— and Suzie I. Tucker, "Allegorical Tradition and the Old English Exodus", *Neophil.*, XLIV (1960), 122-127.

Cyprian, Saint, *Mortality*, ed. and trans. Roy J. Deferrari, V. 36 of *The Fathers of the Church*, 72 vols. (New York, 1947-   ).

Daunt, Marjorie, "Some Difficulties of 'The Seafarer' Reconsidered", *MLR*, XIII (1918), 474-479.

——, " 'The Seafarer', ll. 97-102", *MLR*, XI (1916), 337-338.

Dillistone, F. W., *Christianity and Symbolism* (London, 1955).

Draconti, *Satisfactio*, ed. and trans. Sister M. St. Margaret, Univ. of Pa., dissertation (Philadelphia, 1936).

Dunbar, H. Flanders, *Symbolism in Medieval Thought* (New York, 1961; Rpt. of 1929 ed.).

Dunleavy, Gareth W., *Colum's Other Island: The Irish at Lindisfarne* (Madison, 1960).

Earl, James W., "Christian Tradition in the Old English 'Exodus' ", *NM*, LXXI (1970), 541-570.

Earle, John, *The Deeds of Beowulf* (Oxford, 1892).

Ehrismann, Gustav, "Religionsgeschichtliche Beiträge zum germanischen Fruhcristentum", *Beiträge zur Geschichte der Deutschen Sprache und Literatur*, XXXV (1909), 209-239.

Elliott, R. W. V., *Runes: An Introduction* (Manchester, 1959).

——, "The Wanderer's Conscience", *ES*, XXXIX (1958), 193-200.

Eusebius, Pamphili, *Ecclesiastical History*, trans. Roy J. Deferrari, V. 19 of
  The Fathers of the Church, 72 vols. (New York, 1947-).
——, *The History of the Church*, trans. G. A. Williamson (Baltimore, 1965).
Farrell, Robert T., "A Reading of the O.E. Exodus", *RES*, n.s., XX (1969),
  401-417.
Gerould, Gordon H., "Studies in the Christ", *Engl. Stud.*, XLI (1910), 1-19.
Ginsberg, Louis, *Legends of the Bible* (Philadelphia, 1956).
Gollancz, Sir Israel, ed., *The Caedmon Manuscript* (London, 1927).
——, ed., *The Exeter Book, Part I* (London, 1958; Rpt. of 1895 ed.).
Gordon, I. L., ed., *The Seafarer* (London, 1960).
——, "Traditional Themes in The Wanderer and The Seafarer", *RES*, n.s.,
  V (1954), 1-13.
Gordon, R. K., trans., *Anglo-Saxon Poetry* (London, 1926).
Greenfield, Stanley B., *A Critical History of Old English Literature* (New
  York, 1965).
——, "Attitudes and Values in 'The Seafarer'", *SP*, LI (1954), 15-20.
——, "Of Locks and Keys – Line 19a of the O.E. Christ", *MLN*, LXVII
  (1952), 238-240.
——, "The Theme of Spiritual Exile in 'Christ I'", *PQ*, XXXII (1953), 321-
  328.
——, "The Wanderer: a Reconsideration of Theme and Structure", *JEGP*,
  L (1951), 451-456.
Gregory the Great, Saint, *Dialogues,* trans. Odo John Zimmerman, O.S.B.,
  V. 39 of *The Fathers of the Church*, 72 vols. (New York, 1947-).
Gwynn, Stephen L., *The History of Ireland* (New York, 1923).

Haber, Tom Burns, *A Comparative Study of the Beowulf and the Aeneid*
  (Princeton, 1931).
Hadas, Moses, *A History of Latin Literature* (New York, 1952).
Herben, Stephen J., "The Ruin", *MLN*, LIV (1939), 37-39.
Hodgkin, R. H., *A History of the Anglo-Saxons*, 2 vols., 3rd ed. (London,
  1952).
Hulme, Edward Maslin, *The Middle Ages* (New York, 1929).
Hunt, Theodore W., ed., *Exodus and Daniel* (Boston, 1902).
Huppé, Bernard F., *Doctrine and Poetry* (New York, 1959).
——, "The Wanderer: Theme and Structure", *JEGP*, XLII (1943), 516-538.
Irving, Edward B., Jr., "On the Dating of the Old English Poems *Genesis*
  and *Exodus*", *Anglia*, LXXVII (1959), 1-11.
——, ed., *The Old English Exodus* (New Haven, 1953).

Josephus, *Works*, 2nd ed., trans. William Whiston, intro. by the Rev. H.
  Stebbing (Philadelphia, n.d.).

Keenan, Hugh T., "'Exodus' 312: the Green Street of Paradise", *NM*, LXXI
  (1971), 455-460.
Kennedy, Charles W., trans., *An Anthology of Old English Poetry* (New
  York, 1960).
——, trans., *The Caedmon Poems* (New York, 1916).
——, *The Earliest English Poetry* (New York, 1943).
Kenney, James F., *Sources for the Early History of Ireland*, 2 vols. (New
  York, 1929).

Kershaw, Nora, *Anglo-Saxon and Norse Poems* (Cambridge, 1922).
Klaeber, Frederick, "Die christlichen Elemente im Beowulf", *Anglia*, XXXV
    (1911), 111-136; 249-270; 453-482, and XXXVI (1912), 169-199.
Kluge, Friederich, "Zu altenglischen Dichtungen", *Engl. Stud.*, VIII (1885),
    472-474.
——, "Zu altenglischen Dichtungen: I Der Seefahrer", *Engl. Stud.*, VI (1883),
    322-327.
Krapp, George Philip, ed., *The Junius Manuscript*, V. 1 of *The Anglo-Saxon
    Poetic Records*, 6 vols. (New York, 1931).
—— and Elliott Van Kirk Dobbie, eds., *The Exeter Book*, V. 3 of *The
    Anglo-Saxon Poetic Records*, 6 vols. (New York, 1936).

Lawrence, W. W., "The Wanderer and The Seafarer", *JGP*, IV (1902), 460-
    480.
Leach, Arthur F., *Educational Charters and Documents, 598-1909* (Cam-
    bridge, 1911).
Leslie, R. F., ed., *Three Old English Elegies* (Manchester, 1961).
Liljegren, S. B., "Some Notes on the Old English Poem *The Seafarer*", *Stud.
    Neophil.*, XIV (1941-1942), 145-159.
Lingard, John, *The History and Antiquities of the Anglo-Saxon Church*,
    2nd ed., 2 vols. (London, 1858).
Lucas, Peter J., "The Cloud in the Interpretation of the Old English
    Exodus", *ES*, LI (1970), 297-311.
Lumiansky, R. M., "The Dramatic Structure of the O. E. Wanderer", *Neo-
    phil.*, XXXIV (1956), 104-112.

Mackie, W. S., ed., *The Exeter Book, Part II* (London, 1958; Rpt. of 1895
    ed.).
Malone, Kemp, "On Seafarer 111-116", *MAE*, VI (1937), 214-215.
Meissner, John L. Gough, *The Celtic Church in England after the Synod
    of Whitby* (London, 1929).
Migne, J. P., *Patrologia Cursus Completus*, series latina prima, 221 vols.
    (Paris, 1844-1864).
Mildenberger, Kenneth, "Unity of Cynewulf's Christ in the Light of Icono-
    graphy", *Spec.*, XXIII (1948), 426-432.
Moore, Samuel, "Sources of the Old English Exodus", *MP*, IX (1911), 83-
    103.
——, "The Old English Christ: Is It a Unit?", *JEGP*, XIV (1915), 550-567.
Morris, Richard, ed., *The Blickling Homilies* (London, 1967), Rpt. in 1 vol
    of *EETS* O.S. Nos. 58 (1874), 63 (1876), 73 (1880).
——, ed., *The Blickling Homilies of the Tenth Century* (London, 1880).
Müllenhoff, Karl, *Beowulf* (Berlin, 1889).
Napier, A. S., *Wulfstan* (Weimar, 1882).
Nicoll, W. Robertson, Rev., ed., *The Expositor's Bible*, 25 vols. (New York,
    1903).
Noth, Martin, *Exodus, A Commentary* (Philadelphia, 1962).

Ogilvy, J. D. A., *Books Known to Anglo-Latin Writers from Aldhelm to
    Alcuin (670-804)* (Cambridge, Mass., 1936).
——, *Books Known to the English, 597-1066* (Cambridge, Mass., 1967).

Origen, *Commentary on the Gospel of Matthew*, trans. the Rev. John Patrick, V. 10 of *The Ante-Nicene Fathers*, ed. the Rev. Allan Menzies (Original Supplement to the American Edition) (Grand Rapids, 1969).

Owen, W. J. B., "Wanderer, Lines 50-57", *MLN*, LXV (1950), 161-165.

Peters, Leonard J., "The Relationship Between *Beowulf* and the Old English Andreas", *PMLA*, LXVI (1951), 848-863.

Philip, Bro. Augustine, "The Exeter Scribe and the Unity of the Christ", *PMLA*, LV (1940), 903-909.

Prudentius, Clemens Aurelius, trans. H. J. Thomson, 2 vols. (Cambridge, Mass., 1927).

Raby, F. J. E., *A History of Christian Latin Poetry* (Oxford, 1927).

——, *A History of Christian-Latin Poetry*, 2nd ed. (Oxford, 1953).

——, *A History of Secular Latin Poetry in the Middle Ages* (Oxford, 1957).

Rand, E. K., *Founders of the Middle Ages* (Cambridge, 1928).

Rhys, John, *Studies in the Arthurian Legend* (Oxford, 1891).

Ricci, Aldo, "The Chronology of Anglo-Saxon Poetry", *RES*, V (1929), 257-266.

Rieger, Max, "Der Seefahrer als Dialog hergestehlt", *ZfdP*, I (1869), 334-339.

Robertson, D. W., Jr., "Historical Criticism", *English Institute Essays, 1950* (New York, 1951).

Rumble, Thomas C., "From Eardstapa to Snottor on Mode: the Structural Principle of 'The Wanderer' ", *MLQ*, XIX (1958), 225-230.

Salmon, Vivian, " 'The Wanderer' and 'The Seafarer' and the Old English Conception of the Soul", *MLR*, LV (1960), 1-10.

Savage, Ernest A., *Old English Literature* (Chicago, 1912).

Schaar, Claes, *Critical Studies in the Cynewulf Group* (Lund, 1949).

Schücking, Levin L., Rev. of E. Sieper, *Die altenglische Elegie, Engl. Stud.*, LI (1917), 107.

Sedgefield, W. J., ed., *An Anglo-Saxon Book of Verse and Prose* (Manchester, 1928).

Sisam, Kenneth, "The Seafarer, LL. 72ff.", *Engl. Stud.*, XLVI (1912-1913), 336.

——, *Studies in the History of Old English Literature* (Oxford, 1953).

Smalley, Beryl, *The Study of the Bible in the Middle Ages* (New York, 1952).

Smithers, G. V., "The Meaning of 'The Seafarer' and 'The Wanderer' ", *MAE*, XXVI (1957), 137-153, XXVIII (1959), 1-22.

Stanley, E. G., "Old English Poetic Diction and the Interpretation of The Wanderer, The Seafarer, and The Penitent's Prayer", *Anglia*, LXIII (1955), 413-466.

Stevick, Robert D., "The Text and Composition of the Seafarer", *PMLA*, LXXX (1965), 332-336.

Suddaby, Elizabeth, "Three Notes on Old English Texts", *MLN*, LXIX (1954), 465-468.

Tacitus, *The Agricola and Germany of Tacitus*, trans. Alfred John Church and William Jackson Brodribb (London, 1926).

Taine, H. A., *History of English Literature*, trans. Henri van Laun (New York, 1873).

Teuffel's History of Roman Literature, rev. and enlarged Ludwig Schwabe, trans. George W. Warr, 2 vols. (London, 1900).

Thompson, James Westfall and Edgar Nathaniel Johnson, *An Introduction to Medieval Europe* (New York, 1937).

Thorpe, Benjamin, *Caedmon's Paraphrase* (London, 1832).

—, ed., *The Homilies of the Anglo-Saxon Church*, 2 vols. Aelfric Society, 1844-1846.

Timmer, B. J., "Wyrd in Anglo-Saxon Prose and Poetry", *Neophil.*, XXVI (1941), i, 24-27; ii, 27-33; iii, 213-228.

Trautmann, Moritz, "Der sogenannte Crist", *Anglia*, XVIII (1896), 382-388.

Tucker, Suzie I., "Return to the Wanderer", *EIC*, VIII (1958), 229-237.

Walker, Williston, *A History of the Christian Church* (New York, 1946).

Wardale, E. E., *Chapters on Old English Literature* (London, 1935).

Webber, F. R., *Church Symbolism*, 2nd ed., rev. (Cleveland, 1938).

Whitelock, Dorothy, "The Interpretation of 'The Seafarer'", in *The Early Cultures of North-West Europe*, eds. Sir Cyril Fox and Bruce Dickins (Cambridge, 1950).

Williams, Blanche C., *Gnomic Poetry in Anglo-Saxon* (New York, 1914).

Wood, Cecil, "Nis Þæt Seldguma", *PMLA*, LXXV (1960), 481-484.

Wrenn, C. L., *The Year's Work in English Studies*, XIX (1938).

INDEX

DATE DUE			
NOV 0 7 2001			